S0-DTD-193

1-2-3® Release 2.4
Quick Reference

Que Quick Reference Series

JOYCE J. NIELSEN

1-2-3 Release 2.4 Quick Reference

Copyright ©1992 by Que Corporation.

Library of Congress Catalog Number: 92-81020

ISBN: 0-88022-987-X

95 94 93 92   4 3 2 1

Interpretation of the printing code: the rightmost
double-digit number is the year of the book's printing; the
rightmost single-digit number is the number of the book's
printing. For example, a printing code of 92-4 shows that
the fourth printing of the book occurred in 1992.

Screen reproductions in this book were created using
Collage Plus from Inner Media, Inc., Hollis, NH.

This book is based on 1-2-3 for DOS Release 2.4.

CREDITS

Publisher
Lloyd J. Short

Associate Publisher
Rick Ranucci

Acquisitions Editor
Chris Katsaropoulus

Production Editor
Don Eamon

Editor
Jill D. Bond

Technical Editor
Dave Rourke

Production Team
Mark Enochs
Bob LaRoche
Laurie Lee
Jay Lesandrini
John Sleeva

1-2-3 and Lotus are trademarks of Lotus Development Corporation.

MS-DOS is a trademark of Microsoft Corporation

TABLE OF CONTENTS

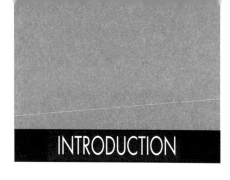

INTRODUCTION

1-2-3 Release 2.4 Quick Reference is a compilation of menu commands, @functions, macro commands, and add-ins available in 1-2-3 Release 2.4. This information is presented in a compact, easy-to-use format that enables you to find the information you need quickly. Most of the information in this quick reference also applies to the earlier 1-2-3 Release 2.3.

1-2-3 Release 2.4 Quick Reference includes separate command references for the 1-2-3 menu commands and the Wysiwyg menu commands. Each command reference is arranged alphabetically, and leads you step-by-step through the commands and procedures for using 1-2-3 Release 2.4 like a pro!

Although *1-2-3 Release 2.4 Quick Reference* contains essential 1-2-3 information, this book isn't intended as a replacement for the comprehensive information presented in a full-size guide. You can supplement this quick reference with one of Que's complete 1-2-3 texts, such as *Using 1-2-3 Release 2.4*, Special Edition.

You now can put essential information at your fingertips with *1-2-3 Release 2.4 Quick Reference*—and the entire Que Quick Reference Series!

HINTS FOR USING THIS BOOK

As you read this book, keep the following conventions in mind:

A - (hyphen) between keys in a key combination indicates that you press and hold the first key while you press the next key. A space between keys in a key combination indicates that you press and release the first key, and then press the next key. Words you type and keys you press appear in boldface blue type.

To select menu options and commands with the mouse, move the pointer to the top of the screen to activate the menu. Then, click on the desired option or command. To select options and commands by using the keyboard, press the keys shown in boldface blue type. Information that appears on-screen is indicated by a special typeface.

WORKSHEET BASICS

Lotus 1-2-3 Release 2.4 is an advanced spreadsheet that also contains spreadsheet publishing and presentation features. You can use 1-2-3 Release 2.4 to perform calculations, analyze data, manage files, publish reports, create graphs, and automate routine tasks by using macros.

You can use 1-2-3 commands for copying or moving portions of the worksheet, formatting cells to display currency, and using the database. You access 1-2-3 commands through multilevel menus or the new SmartIcons included in 1-2-3 Release 2.4 (discussed in a following section). Some menus and commands ask you to enter text or cell-address information. Other prompts require only that you type text. After you supply an answer to a prompt, press Enter.

The *command line*, the second line on-screen, displays the current menu selections. To select a menu item, press ← or → (or the space bar) until the desired choice is highlighted, and press Enter. For a quicker method, type the first character of the menu item. You also can select menu options with a mouse, by clicking the desired menu options.

As you use 1-2-3, watch the *prompt line*, which is the third line on-screen. This line displays the next level of menu options or a brief description of the high-lighted menu option. If you make an incorrect selection from a menu, press Esc to return to the preceding menu.

1-2-3 KEYS

Direction Keys

The *direction keys* (or *pointer-movement keys*) move the cell pointer in the worksheet. Many of these keys also move the cursor in EDIT mode. Press Num Lock to toggle between directional movement and numeric-keypad entry.

The following table lists and describes the direction keys:

Key(s)	Description
←	Moves the cell pointer left one cell.
→	Moves the cell pointer right one cell.
↑	Moves the cell pointer up one cell.

Key(s)	Description
↓	Moves the cell pointer down one cell.
End ←	Moves the cell pointer to the left.*
End →	Moves the cell pointer to the right.*
End ↑	Moves the cell pointer up.*
End ↓	Moves the cell pointer down.*
End Home	Moves the cell pointer to the lower right corner of the active area of the worksheet.
Home	Moves the cell pointer to the home position (cell A1, unless you set titles by using /Worksheet Titles).
PgUp	Moves the cell pointer up one screen.
PgDn	Moves the cell pointer down one screen.
Shift-Tab or Ctrl ←	Moves the cell pointer left one screen.
Tab or Ctrl →	Moves the cell pointer right one screen.
F5 (GoTo)	Moves the cell pointer directly to cell address or range name you specify.
F6 (Window)	If the window is split, moves the cell pointer to the other window.

* *Moves the cell pointer in the direction of the arrow to the next intersection between a blank cell and a cell that contains data.*

Function Keys

Function keys save time as you perform special tasks. Depending on the hardware, function keys are labeled F1 through F10. Some keyboards have twelve function keys. 1-2-3 uses only the first ten.

The following table lists function keys and their descriptions:

Key(s)	Description
F1 (Help)	Accesses the on-line Help facility.
F2 (Edit)	Places 1-2-3 in EDIT mode so that you can change the current cell; also enables you to activate a dialog box.
F3 (Name)	Displays a list of names any time a command or formula can accept a range name or a file name.
F4 (Abs)	Changes a cell or range address from relative to absolute to mixed and back to relative; in READY mode, enables you to prespecify ranges in 1-2-3 or Wysiwyg.
F5 (GoTo)	Moves the cell pointer to a specified cell address or range name.
F6 (Window)	Moves the cell pointer to the other window when the screen is split; also toggles the dialog box display.
F7 (Query)	In READY mode, repeats the last /Data Query command. During a /Data Query Find, switches between FIND and READY modes.

Key(s)	Description
F8 (Table)	Repeats the last /Data Table command.
F9 (Calc)	In READY mode, recalculates the worksheet. If entering or editing a formula, converts the formula to its current value.
F10 (Graph)	Displays the current graph. If no current graph exists, displays a blank screen.
Alt-F1 (Compose)	Creates international characters that cannot be typed directly by using the keyboard.
Alt-F2 (Step)	Activates STEP mode, enabling you to execute macros one step at a time; acts as a toggle.
Alt-F3 (Run)	Displays a list of range names in the worksheet, enabling you to select the name of a macro to run.
Alt-F4 (Undo)	Reverses the last action (if Undo is enabled).
Alt-F5 (Learn)	Activates the Learn feature and begins recording keystrokes you specified in a learn range by selecting /Worksheet Learn Range; press Alt-F5 again to stop recording keystrokes.
Alt-F6	Not used in 1-2-3 Release 2.x.
Alt-F7 (App1)	Starts a 1-2-3 add-in, if assigned to this key.
Alt-F8 (App2)	Starts a 1-2-3 add-in, if assigned to this key.

continues

Key(s)	Description
Alt-F9 (App3)	Starts a 1-2-3 add-in, if assigned to this key.
Alt-F10 (App4)	Starts a 1-2-3 add-in, if assigned to this key; otherwise, displays /Add-In menu.
Ctrl-F1 (Bookmark)	Displays the last Help screen viewed.

Special Keys

The special keys provide important 1-2-3 functions. Some special keys change the actions of other keys and act as a toggle.

The following table lists special keys and their descriptions:

Key	Description
/ or <	Generates the 1-2-3 main menu in READY mode. The slash also is used as a division sign when you enter data or edit a formula in a cell. The less-than sign also is used as a less-than symbol in formulas.
:	Generates the Wysiwyg main menu when Wysiwyg is in memory.
. (period)	Separates the address of the cell at the beginning of the range from the address of the cell at the end of the range when used in a range address. Moves the anchor cell to another corner of the range in POINT mode.

Key	Description
Backspace	Erases the preceding character during data entry or editing. Cancels old ranges that appear in some prompts. If you are using Help, displays the preceding Help screen.
Ctrl-Break	Cancels a macro or cancels menu choices and returns 1-2-3 to READY mode.
Del	Erases the cell entry (similar to /Range Erase) when a cell that contains an entry is highlighted; deletes one character at the cursor when editing a cell.
Esc	Cancels the current menu and returns to the preceding menu when accessing the command menus. Clears the edit line when you enter or edit data in a cell. Cancels a range during some prompts that display the old range. Returns to READY mode from the on-line Help facility. Clears error messages.
Ins	Changes mode to overtype when editing a cell. Press Ins again to return to insert mode.
Num Lock	Toggles the numeric keypad from directional movement to numeric entry.
Scroll Lock	Toggles the scroll function on and off; scrolls the entire window (when active) when you press an arrow key.

USING A MOUSE

You use the mouse to navigate the 1-2-3 screen and to select items.

To click an item

Position the mouse pointer on the item and then press and release the left mouse button.

To double-click an item

Position the mouse pointer on the item and then click the left mouse button twice in rapid succession.

To drag an item

Position the mouse pointer on the item. Press and hold down the left mouse button, and then slide the mouse across a flat surface to move the item to a different location.

You can use a mouse with 1-2-3 Releases 2.3 and 2.4 if you installed the mouse driver. In Release 2.3, Wysiwyg also must be in memory. To install the mouse driver, refer to the documentation that came with the mouse. To install Wysiwyg, use the procedure outlined at the beginning of the Wysiwyg Command Reference section in this book.

Reminder: When you move the mouse pointer to the control panel, the 1-2-3 menu, or the Wysiwyg menu you last used appears. Click the right mouse button to toggle between these menus.

To move the cell pointer by using the mouse

To move the cell pointer to a cell with the mouse, click the desired cell with the left mouse button.

You also can move the cell pointer by clicking the arrow SmartIcons that appear in the SmartIcon palette. Click the arrows with the left mouse button to move the cell pointer in the direction that an arrow points in a worksheet. If you click an arrow SmartIcon once, the cell pointer moves to the next cell. Press and hold the left mouse button to scroll continuously. To stop scrolling, release the mouse button.

To select menu commands by using the mouse

You can use the mouse to select commands from either the 1-2-3 menu or the Wysiwyg menu.

1. Move the mouse pointer to the control panel.

2. To switch to the opposite menu (if necessary), click the right mouse button.

3. Use the left mouse button to click the desired command(s).

To specify a range by using the mouse

1. When prompted to enter a range, position the mouse pointer on a corner cell of the range to specify.

2. Drag the mouse pointer to the opposite corner of the range and release the button.

   If you decide to cancel the highlighted range, click the right mouse button or press Esc.

3. To finish specifying the range, click the left mouse button again.

To prespecify a range by using a mouse

You can highlight a range before you select a menu command. This technique is particularly helpful when using multiple formatting commands on a single range.

1. Position the mouse pointer on a corner cell of the range to specify.

2. Click and hold the left mouse button and drag the mouse pointer to the opposite corner of the range; release the button.

3. Select one or more commands to affect the selected range.

4. To return to READY mode, press Esc, move the cell pointer, or click the left mouse button.

USING SMARTICONS

The SmartIcons add-in provided with 1-2-3 Release 2.4 offers instant access to the most commonly used 1-2-3 and Wysiwyg commands and procedures. SmartIcons are a graphical technique for making software easier to use.

In 1-2-3 Release 2.4, the SmartIcons represent 1-2-3 actions or commands. To execute a command, point to a SmartIcon with the mouse pointer and quickly press (*click*) the left mouse button.

To use the SmartIcons with the keyboard, hold the Alt key and press the function key assigned during installation (usually F7), which highlights the first SmartIcon on the current palette. To select a SmartIcon, press ↑ or ↓ to move the highlight in the current palette. To move between SmartIcon palettes, press → or ←. Press Enter to select the highlighted SmartIcon.

The SmartIcons add-in installs like the other 1-2-3 add-in programs. When you install 1-2-3 Release 2.4 for the first time, however, the Install program copies the SmartIcons and sets up 1-2-3 to attach SmartIcons each time you use 1-2-3.

Understanding SmartIcons

SmartIcons are pictures that appear on the right side of the 1-2-3 screen, arranged in several *palettes*. The total number of palettes depends on the resolution of the graphics monitor and on whether Wysiwyg is attached.

To view a description of a SmartIcon, point to the SmartIcon with the mouse pointer and press the right mouse button. A description appears in the 1-2-3 control panel.

The SmartIcons are arranged on several palettes. The current SmartIcon palette number is indicated at the bottom of the SmartIcon palette. On either side of the number is an arrow. You use these arrows to switch between SmartIcon palettes; point to the appropriate arrow and click the mouse to change palettes. Click the right arrow to move to the next palette or click the left arrow to move to the previous palette.

The SmartIcons look best in Wysiwyg graphics mode, the default mode for 1-2-3 when the Wysiwyg add-in is attached. The SmartIcons look better in graphics mode because Wysiwyg uses the graphics capability of the screen to display the SmartIcon image.

SmartIcons also can be used with 1-2-3 in text mode. 1-2-3 is in text mode when the Wysiwyg add-in isn't attached or when the Wysiwyg display option is set for text. 1-2-3 cannot display the graphic pictures in text mode, so the program uses letters, numbers, and ASCII drawing characters to depict the SmartIcons.

SmartIcons Descriptions

The following table displays the SmartIcons in graphics mode and briefly describes the function of each SmartIcon.

The 1-2-3 SmartIcons

SmartIcon	Description
	Saves the current worksheet
U	Underlines
U	Double underlines
$	Applies Currency 2 format
0,0	Applies , (comma) 0 format
%	Applies Percent 2 format
ᴬA	Cycles through fonts
AA	Cycles through colors
AA	Cycles through colors for background
❑	Outlines and adds drop shadow
☐	Outlines
▦	Applies light shading
≡	Left-aligns
≡	Center-aligns
≡	Right-aligns
▦	Changes text alignment in a range of cells
▦	Inserts row(s)
▦	Inserts column(s)
▦	Deletes selected row(s)

SmartIcon	Description
	Deletes selected column(s)
	Inserts horizontal (row) page break
	Inserts vertical (column) page break
	Sorts in ascending order
	Sorts in descending order
	Fills range with a sequence of values
	Recalculates formulas
	Enters current date
	Circles highlighted cell or range
	Changes display size of worksheet
	Turns on STEP mode
	Selects and runs a macro
	Moves the cell pointer left one cell
	Moves the cell pointer right one cell
	Moves the cell pointer up one cell
	Moves the cell pointer down one cell
	Displays Help information
	Equivalent of pressing Home
	Equivalent of pressing End Home
	Equivalent of pressing End ($\downarrow$)
	Equivalent of pressing End ($\uparrow$)
	Equivalent of pressing End ($\rightarrow$)
	Equivalent of pressing End ($\leftarrow$)
	Goes to a cell or range
	Searches and/or replaces

continues

SmartIcon	Description
	Undoes the last command or action
	Erases the highlighted range
	Retrieves an existing worksheet
	Sums the nearest adjacent range
	Graphs the current range
	Adds current graph to worksheet
	Displays current graph
	Enters text edit mode
	Prints the highlighted range
	Previews the print range
	Selects the range to copy to
	Selects the range to move to
	Selects the range to apply current formats to
	Copies current cell to selected cells
B	Adds or removes boldface
I	Adds or removes italics
N	Normal (removes Wysiwyg formatting)
	Adds SmartIcon to custom palette
	Deletes SmartIcon from custom palette
	Rearranges SmartIcons on custom palette
	Attaches macro to user SmartIcon
U1	User SmartIcon #1
U2	User SmartIcon #2

SmartIcon	Description
U3	User SmartIcon #3
U4	User SmartIcon #4
U5	User SmartIcon #5
U6	User SmartIcon #6
U7	User SmartIcon #7
U8	User SmartIcon #8
U9	User SmartIcon #9
U10	User SmartIcon #10
U11	User SmartIcon #11
U12	User SmartIcon #12

Customizing SmartIcons

You can customize SmartIcons in two ways. You can add SmartIcons to the first SmartIcon palette so that the SmartIcons you use most often are available on the same palette. 1-2-3 also offers 12 user SmartIcons to which you can attach macros that you create.

Using the Custom Palette

The first SmartIcon palette is the *custom palette*. You can add or delete SmartIcons on this palette. You cannot modify the SmartIcons that appear on any other palette.

To add SmartIcons to the custom palette, switch SmartIcon palettes until you see the Add Icon and Delete Icon SmartIcons. (To identify how these SmartIcons appear, look for the descriptions in the preceding table and view the associated graphic of these SmartIcons.) These special SmartIcons add and delete other SmartIcons on the custom palette.

To add SmartIcons to the custom palette, follow these steps:

1. Select the Add Icon SmartIcon.

   The first SmartIcon on the current palette is highlighted and a message box appears on-screen. If you have a mouse, the message box instructs you to use the mouse to select the SmartIcon to add to the custom palette. If you don't have a mouse, the message box prompts you to use the arrow keys to select a SmartIcon to add to the custom palette.

2. Use the mouse or the keyboard to select the SmartIcon to add to the custom palette.

To delete SmartIcons from the custom palette, select the Delete Icon SmartIcon. The custom palette appears. With the mouse or the keyboard, select a SmartIcon to delete.

Attaching Macros to SmartIcons

A powerful feature of SmartIcons is the capability of attaching macros to SmartIcons. These programmable SmartIcons are referred to as *user SmartIcons*; 12 user SmartIcons are available. You can program the SmartIcons to perform commonly used tasks or to make 1-2-3 applications easier to use.

You see the user SmartIcons on the last SmartIcon palette, labeled U1 through U12. You cannot change the appearance of user SmartIcons, but you can add these icons to the custom palette.

To attach a macro to a user SmartIcon, follow these steps:

1. Select the User Icon SmartIcon. The User Icon Descriptions dialog box appears.

2. Select a user SmartIcon number to assign a macro.

3. Select Assign Macro to Icon to display the User-Defined Icon dialog box.

4. Select Icon Description and enter a description to appear when the SmartIcon is selected. This description may be up to 72 characters in length.

5. Select Macro Text and enter the macro text in the text box. You can enter up to 240 characters in the text box.

   You also can select Source Range to copy the macro text from the worksheet. Specify a cell, a range of cells, or a range name for the macro in this box. If you have a macro named \a, for example, type \a in this box. You can press F4 to enter POINT mode to select the cell from the worksheet or press F3 (Name) to select a range name from a list of range names. Select Get Macro from Sheet to copy the macro into the macro text box.

6. To copy the macro to the user SmartIcon, select OK in the User-Defined Icon dialog box. To exit without attaching the macro, select Cancel.

The actual keystrokes, not the range name or cell address, appear in the Macro Text field in the dialog box. 1-2-3 reads the macro from the worksheet into the SmartIcon definition from the cell or range specified. To copy text from more than one cell, you must select the entire range.

ENTERING AND EDITING DATA

The following sections discuss how to enter labels (text), numbers, and formulas in a cell. You also learn how to modify existing cell contents.

After you type the first character of a cell entry, 1-2-3 determines the format of the entry. When the entry is text, the mode indicator changes to LABEL. When the entry is the beginning of a number or formula, the mode indicator changes to VALUE.

Entering Labels

To enter a label

Type the label into the cell. If the label starts with one of the following numeric characters, make sure that you precede the label with a label prefix. The label prefix tells 1-2-3 that the entry is a label and indicates how the text is aligned in the cell. If you don't start the entry with a label prefix and the entry begins with one of the numeric characters, 1-2-3 considers the entry a value.

0 1 2 3 4 5 6 7 8 9 . + - $ (@ #

Notes

The following table lists label prefixes you can use to control alignment:

Label Prefix	Description
' (apostrophe)	Aligns a label to the left (default setting).
" (quotation mark)	Aligns a label to the right.
^ (caret)	Centers a label in a cell.
\ (backslash)	Repeats a character to fill a cell.*
| (vertical bar)	Aligns a label to the left; doesn't print the label when you print the work-sheet in the first column of the print range.*
"" (double quotes)	Aligns a label to the right in Wysiwyg.*
^^ (double caret)	Centers a label in the cell in Wysiwyg.*

*You cannot select this prefix with /**W**orksheet **G**lobal **L**abel-Prefix or /**R**ange **L**abel.*

Select /Worksheet Global Label-Prefix to change the default label prefix. This command changes only new labels. To change the alignment of existing labels, select /Range Label.

Entering Numbers

To enter a number

Begin the entry with one of the following characters:

0 1 2 3 4 5 6 7 8 9 . + - $

If you begin the entry with any other character, 1-2-3 assumes that the entry is a label or a formula.

Entering Formulas

To enter a formula

Begin the entry with one of the following characters:

0 1 2 3 4 5 6 7 8 9 . + - $ (@ #

If you begin the entry with any other character, 1-2-3 assumes that the entry is a label.

Use operators to specify the calculations that you want 1-2-3 to perform. Use parentheses to change the order of precedence (the order in which the operators are evaluated).

Notes

Numeric formulas operate on numbers, string formulas operate on text, and logical formulas compare two entries. The result of a logical test is TRUE or FALSE. TRUE has a value of 1, and FALSE has a value of 0.

You may include the following items in formulas:

Item	Description
@functions	Predefined formulas
Addresses	Cell addresses or range names
Operators	Symbols, such as + and –, for numeric, string, or logical operations
Numbers	Used for math calculations
Strings	Text used in string formulas

The following table lists, describes, and ranks the order of precedence of the numeric operators:

Operator	Description	Precedence
^	Exponentiation	1
+, –	Positive, negative	2
*, /	Multiplication, division	3
+, –	Addition, subtraction	4
=, <>	Equal, not equal	5
<, >	Less than, greater than	5
<=	Less than or equal to	5
>=	Greater than or equal to	5
#NOT#	Logical NOT	6
#AND#	Logical AND	7
#OR#	Logical OR	7

The following table lists and describes string operators:

Operator	Description
+	Begins a formula that starts with a cell address or a text string.
&	Concatenates a string to the preceding string (adds second string to the end of the first string).

To place a string inside a formula, enclose the string in double quotes.

Editing Cell Contents

You can press Backspace to correct a typing error while you enter data. Press F2 (Edit) to modify long entries or existing cell contents.

To write over existing cell contents

Type a new entry; the new entry replaces the old entry when you press Enter. To cancel the new entry and keep the old entry, press Esc before pressing Enter.

To edit cell contents

1. Highlight the cell you want to edit.
2. Press F2 (Edit).

   The cell contents appear on the second line on-screen. The cursor indicates where the typed information is placed.

3. Use the editing keys to make changes. The editing keys include the left- and right-arrow keys, Tab, Shift-Tab, Home, End, Del, Ins, and Backspace.

4. After editing, press Enter (the cursor can be anywhere in the edit line at this time).

1-2-3 COMMAND REFERENCE

The 1-2-3 Command Reference includes all the available 1-2-3 commands when you press / (slash). These commands are presented alphabetically.

Each command is followed by an explanation of its purpose and reminders of any preparation required before you activate the command. The procedures are indicated in a step-by-step manner. Keystrokes within the text you type are in boldface blue. A notes section contains additional comments, information, hints, or suggestions for using the command.

Note

When you type the designated letter to select a command, you don't have to capitalize the letter.

/Add-In Attach

Purpose

Loads an add-in application program in memory. Add-in applications are programs that work with 1-2-3 to extend the capabilities of the program. Release 2.4 comes with seven add-in programs: Auditor, Backsolver, Macro Library Manager, SmartIcons, Tutor, Viewer, and Wysiwyg.

With this command, you assign a function key, such as Alt-F7, which you invoke each time you want to use the add-in.

Reminder: The 1-2-3 Install program by default installs add-ins in the 1-2-3 program directory. 1-2-3 by default looks to this directory for add-ins.

To load an add-in program into memory

1. Select /Add-In Attach.
2. Highlight the add-in name in the list of ADN files that appears. Press Enter.
3. Select 7, 8, 9, or 10 to assign the add-in to one of the Alt-F7 through Alt-F10 key combinations. No-Key doesn't assign the add-in to any function key; the add-in must be invoked by using /Add-In Invoke.

Notes

To have an add-in attach to 1-2-3 each time you start the program with the command /Worksheet Global Default Other Add-in Set, be sure that you select /Worksheet Global Default Update to save the setting.

When no memory is available to attach an add-in, you see a MEMORY FULL message. Depending on the amount of memory or the size of the worksheet, invoking an add-in may disable the Undo feature. You can remove from memory any add-ins you already have attached by using /Add-In Detach, which makes room for the other add-in. You can exit 1-2-3 and free memory by removing other memory-resident programs.

/Add-In Detach/Clear

Purpose

Removes add-ins from memory to free more memory for worksheets or other add-ins.

Reminder: If you used /Worksheet Global Default
Other Add-In Set, the add-in is attached automati-
cally when 1-2-3 is loaded. Otherwise, you must use
/Add-In Attach to attach the add-in.

To remove one add-in from memory
1. Select /Add-In Detach.
2. Highlight the attached add-in from the list that appears on-screen. Press Enter.
3. Select Quit to leave the Add-In menu.

To remove all add-ins from memory
1. Select /Add-In Clear.
2. Select Quit to leave the Add-In menu.

Note
The /Add-In Detach and /Add-In Clear commands
remove the applications from memory during the
current work session only. To remove an auto-
attached add-in, use /Worksheet Global Default
Other Add-In Cancel. Be sure that you use
/Worksheet Global Default Update to save the
setting.

/Add-In Invoke

Purpose
Activates an add-in program you attached previ-
ously. Use this command to use the commands
available in the add-in program, if you haven't
assigned an Alt-key combination.

Reminder: You must attach the add-in to 1-2-3 by using /Add-In Attach or, if you used /Worksheet Global Default Other Add-In Set, the add-in attaches when 1-2-3 loads.

To activate an add-in without using an assigned function key combination
1. Select /Add-In Invoke.
2. Highlight the add-in from the list of attached add-ins and press Enter.

To activate an add-in by using an assigned function key combination
Press the Alt-*function key* combination you assigned to the add-in. If you assigned F7 to the add-in, for example, press Alt-F7 to invoke the add-in.

Notes
Refer to the add-in documentation for specific use instructions.

You can, by default, attach and invoke an add-in each time you start 1-2-3 with the /Worksheet Global Default Other Add-In Set command. Answer Yes to the prompt Automatically invoke this add-in when you start 1-2-3. To save the setting, use /Worksheet Global Default Update.

/Copy

Purpose
Copies formulas, values, labels, formats, and cell-protection attributes to new locations.

> **Reminder:** Make sure that you have enough space on the worksheet to receive the cell or range being copied. The copy replaces the contents of the destination (the cell or cells being copied).

To copy data

1. Select /Copy.
2. The Copy what? prompt requests the range of the cells to copy. 1-2-3 shows the location of the cell pointer as the default. Highlight a range, or type the range name or the range address. Press Enter.
3. At the To where? prompt, specify the upper left corner where you want the duplicate to appear by moving the cell pointer to that position, or by typing the cell address or range name. Then press Enter.

/Data Distribution

Purpose

Creates a frequency distribution of the values in a specified range.

> **Reminder:** This command works only on numeric values.

You must arrange the data in a column, row, or rectangular range known as the *value range*.

Move the cell pointer to a worksheet portion that has two adjacent blank columns. In the left column, enter the interval values as a *bin range* in ascending order.

To create a frequency distribution

1. Select /Data Distribution.
2. Enter the value range, which contains the data being analyzed and press Enter.
3. Enter the bin range and press Enter.

Note

The frequency distribution appears in the column to the right of the bin range. The frequency column extends one row beyond the bin range.

/Data Fill

Purpose

Fills a specified range with a series of equally incremented numbers, dates, times, or percentages.

Use /Data Fill to create date rows or columns, numeric rows or columns, headings for depreciation tables, sensitivity analyses, data tables, or databases.

> **Reminder:** The numbers generated overwrite previous contents of the cells within the range.

To fill a range

1. Select /Data Fill.
2. Specify the range to fill and press Enter.
3. Enter the start number, date, or time in the filled range and press Enter. The default value is 0.
4. When a Step value is requested, type the positive or negative number by which you want to increment the value and press Enter. The default value is 1.
5. Enter a Stop value and press Enter.

/Data Matrix

Purpose

Inverts columns and rows in square matrices.
Multiplies column-and-row matrices of cells.

To invert a matrix

1. Select /Data Matrix.

2. Select Invert to invert a square matrix of up to
   80 rows and columns.

3. Specify the worksheet range to invert and
   press Enter.

4. Specify an output range in the worksheet to
   hold the inverted solution matrix and press
   Enter.

Note

/DMI creates a matrix the same size as the matrix
you are inverting. Make sure that you specify a
worksheet area large enough to hold the matrix and
verify that the area contains no data that you may
not want overwritten.

To multiply matrices

1. Select /Data Matrix.

2. Select Multiply and specify the first range to
   multiply; then specify the second range to
   multiply and press Enter. The number of columns in the first matrix must be equal to the
   number of columns in the second matrix.

3. Highlight the upper left corner of the output
   range and press Enter.

/Data Parse

Purpose

Separates long labels that result from the /File Import Text command into distinct text and numeric cell entries. The separated text and numbers are placed in individual cells in a row of an output range.

To parse data

1. Move the cell pointer to the first cell in the row where you want to begin parsing.

2. Select /Data Parse.

3. Select Format-Line.

4. Select Create. A format line is inserted at the cell pointer, and the row of data moves down. This format line displays 1-2-3's *best guess* at how to separate the data in the cell.

5. To change the format line to include or exclude data (if necessary), select Edit from the Format-Line menu. Edit the format line and press Enter.

6. If the imported data is in different formats—an uneven number of items or a mixture of field names and numbers—you must create additional format lines. Enter these lines at the row where the data format changed.

7. Select Input-Column. Be sure that you specify the entire column of data that you want to parse.

8. Specify the column that contains the format line and the data to format.

9. Select Output-Range.

10. Move the cell pointer to the upper left corner of the range to receive the parsed data and press Enter. Make sure that the range is large enough and doesn't contain data that you don't want overwritten.

11. Select Go.

Note

Select /Data Parse Reset to clear the Input column or Output range text boxes.

/Data Query Criteria

Purpose

Specifies the worksheet range that contains the criteria that defines which records to find.

Reminder: You must specify a criteria range before you use the Find, Extract, Unique, or Delete options of the /Data Query command.

To specify a criteria range

1. Select /Data Query Criteria.

2. Specify or highlight the range that you want to contain field names and criteria.

   The range must contain at least two rows. The first row includes field names from the top row of the database to search and the second row includes the criteria you specify.

/Data Query Delete

Purpose

Removes from the input range any records that meet conditions in the criteria range.

"Cleans up" a database by removing records that aren't current or that you extracted to another worksheet.

Reminders: You must define a 1-2-3 database with input, criteria, and output ranges before you use /Data Query Delete.

Use /Data Query Find to ensure that the criteria is accurate before you delete those records that meet the specified conditions.

To remove database records

1. Select /Data Query Delete.
2. Select Delete to remove the records from the input range, or select Cancel to stop the command without deleting records.

   If you choose Delete, the records are deleted and the database range adjusted.

/Data Query Extract/Unique

Purpose

Copies to the output range of the worksheet records that meet conditions set in the criteria. With /Data Query Unique, 1-2-3 copies only nonduplicate records.

Reminder: You must define a 1-2-3 database with input, output, and criteria ranges before you use /Data Query Extract/Unique.

To copy records

Select /Data Query Extract to copy all records that meet the conditions set in the criteria.

Select /Data Query Unique to copy nonduplicate records that meet conditions set in the criteria and to sort the copied records.

/Data Query Find

Purpose

Finds records in the database that meet conditions you set in the criteria range.

> **Reminder:** You must define a 1-2-3 database with input, output, and criteria ranges before you use /Data Query Find.

To find database records

1. Select /Data Query Find.

   The cell pointer highlights the entire first record that meets the criteria.

   You hear a beep if no record in the input range meets the criteria.

2. Press ↑ or ↓ to move to the next record that meets the criteria. 1-2-3 beeps if you cannot go farther, and Home and End moves you to the first or last record of the database, regardless of whether it meets the criteria.

3. You can edit contents within a record. When the cell pointer highlights the record you want to edit, press F2 and then press ← or → to move the cell you want to edit. Edit the cell contents and press Enter.

/Data Query Input

Purpose

Specifies a range of data records to search.

Reminders: You must specify an input range before you use the Find, Extract, Unique, or Delete
options of the /Data Query command.

The input range can be the entire database or a
portion of the database, and must include the field
names.

To specify a range of records to search

1. Select /Data Query Input.

2. Specify the range of data records to search. Be
   sure that you include in the range the field
   names at the top of the range and portions of
   the records that may be off the screen.

3. After you specify the database, press Enter.

/Data Query Output

Purpose

Assigns a location to which found records can be
copied by using the Extract or Unique commands.

Reminder: You must indicate an output range
before you use the Extract or Unique options of
the /Data Query command. The Find and Delete
options don't use an output range.

To specify an output range

1. Select /Data Query Output.

2. Highlight the range of output field names.

   When you specify only the row of field headings as the output range, 1-2-3 immediately
   erases all data under them, all the way to the

bottom of the worksheet. To avoid accidentally erasing data, you can specify an output
range large enough to contain the extracted
data.

/Data Regression

Purpose

Finds trends in data by using multiple linear regression techniques.

Reminder: The output area must be at least nine
rows and must be two columns wider than the
number of sets of x values (no less than four
columns wide).

To find trends in data

1. Select /Data Regression.

2. Select X-Range, and then specify the range,
   which can contain a maximum of 16 columns
   of independent variables, and then press
   Enter. The values must be in adjacent
   columns.

3. Select Y-Range and specify the range that contains a single column of dependent variables.
   This single column must contain the same
   number of rows as the X-range.

4. Select Intercept, and then select Compute or
   Zero.

5. Select Output-Range and enter the cell address
   of the upper left corner of the output range.

6. Select Go to calculate the regression.

Note

Select Reset from the Regression menu to clear all
specified ranges.

/Data Sort

Purpose

Sorts the database in ascending or descending order.

> **Reminders:** Sorting can be done on one or more fields (columns).
>
> Don't include blank rows or the field headings at the top of the database when you highlight the data range. Blank rows sort to the top or bottom of the database, and the field headings sort into the body of the database.

To sort a database

1. Select /Data Sort Data-Range.
2. Highlight the data range you want to sort. You must include every field (column) in the database, but don't include the field headings at the top of the database (which causes the headings to be sorted with the data). Press Enter.
3. Select Primary-Key.
4. Move the cell pointer to the column of the database that will be the Primary-Key, and then press Enter.
5. Specify Ascending or Descending order.
6. Select the Secondary-Key if you want to sort duplicate copies of the Primary-Key.
7. Specify Ascending or Descending order.
8. Select Go to sort the database.

/Data Table 1/2

Purpose

Generates a table composed of one or two varying input values and formulas. These commands are useful for generating *what-if* models.

> **Reminder:** Use /Data Table 1 to show how changes in one variable affect the output from one or more formulas. Use /Data Table 2 to show how changes in two variables affect the output from one formula.

To create a data table

1. Select /Data Table.
2. Select 1 or 2.

   If you select 1, enter the table range so that it includes the Input 1 values or text in the extreme left column and the formulas in the top row.

   If you select 2, enter the table range so that it includes the Input 1 values or text in the extreme left column and the Input 2 values or text in the top row.

3. Enter the address for Input 1.

   For /Data Table 2, enter the address for Input 2.

1-2-3 places the Input value(s) in the designated cell(s), recalculates each formula, and places the results in the data table.

/File Admin Link-Refresh

Purpose

Recalculates formulas in the current file that depend on data in other files.

Ensures that the worksheet is using current data when the files are shared between users (on a network, for example).

> **Reminder:** If the current file is linked to other files that might have changed, use /File Admin Link-Refresh before printing or reviewing final results.

To recalculate formulas that depend on data in other files

Select /File Admin Link-Refresh.

/File Admin Reservation

Purpose

Controls the reservation status of a shared file on a network. A reservation is the capability of writing to a file with the same file name.

To modify the reservation status of a shared file

1. Select /File Admin Reservation.
2. Select Get or Release to obtain or give up the reservation status of a shared file.

   If you don't have the file reservation, RO for Read Only appears in the status line.

/File Admin Table

Purpose

Enters a table of information (file name, date, time, and size) for the selected file type into the worksheet.

To enter a table of file information into a worksheet

1. Select /File Admin Table.
2. Select Worksheet, Print, Graph, Other, or Linked.
3. If you select Worksheet, Print, Graph, or Other, press Enter to enter a table for the current directory. If you want a table from another directory, press Esc to clear entry; then type the directory name and press Enter.
4. Highlight the upper left corner of the range where you want to place the table and press Enter.

/File Combine

Purpose

Combines values or formulas from a file or worksheet on-disk into the current file.

Reminder: Use /File Combine to copy the contents from the file on disk to the current file, to add values from the file on disk to values or blank cells in the current file, and to subtract incoming values from the numeric values or blank cells in the current file.

To combine values or formulas

1. Place the cell pointer in the upper left corner of the range where you want to combine the data.
2. Select /File Combine.
3. Select Copy, Add, or Subtract.
4. Select Entire-File or Named/Specified-Range.
5. If you select Named/Specified-Range, you are asked to enter the range name (or the range address), then you must select a file name from the list displayed in the control panel. If you select Entire-File, select a file name from the list displayed in the control panel. Press Enter.

/File Directory

Purpose

Changes the current disk drive or directory for the current work session.

To change the current disk drive or directory

1. Select /File Directory.
2. If the drive and directory that appear are correct, press Enter.
3. To change the settings, you can type a new drive letter and directory name at the prompt or edit the existing one and press Enter.

/File Erase

Purpose

Erases files from disk so that you have more available disk space.

> **Reminder:** You cannot restore an erased file.
> Be sure that you will not need a file before you
> erase it.

To erase a file

1. Select /File Erase.
2. Select Worksheet, Print, Graph, or Other to
   specify the type of file you want to erase.
3. Type the path and the name of the file, or use
   the arrow keys to highlight the file you want to
   erase. Press Enter.
4. Select Yes or No from the menu to verify that
   you do or don't want to erase the file.

/File Import

Purpose

Brings ASCII text files into 1-2-3 worksheets.

> **Reminder:** Remember that /File Import can be
> used in two ways to transfer data into a 1-2-3
> worksheet. The first method reads each row of
> ASCII characters as left-aligned labels in a column.
> The second method reads text enclosed in quota-
> tion marks or numbers surrounded by spaces or
> separated by commas into separate cells.

To import ASCII files

1. Move the cell pointer to the upper left corner
   of the range in which you want to import data.
2. Select /File Import. 1-2-3 by default looks for
   files with a PRN extension.

3. To import the ASCII file, select Text or Numbers.

4. Select the ASCII print file. Press Enter. The ASCII file appears in the worksheet.

Note

Each imported line is limited to a length of 240 characters.

/File List

Purpose

Displays all file names of a specific type stored on the current drive and directory or on the drive and directory that you specify. Displays the size of the file (in bytes) and the date and time the file was created. Also displays all files to which the current file is linked.

To display a list of files

1. Select /File List.

2. To specify the type of file you want to display, select Worksheet, Print, Graph, Other, or Linked.

3. Use the arrow keys to highlight individual file names and to display specific information.

4. If you choose anything other than Link, to display files from a different directory, select another directory name.

   Press Backspace to move to a parent directory.

5. Press Enter to return to the worksheet.

/File Retrieve

Purpose

Loads the requested worksheet file from disk into memory.

Reminder: The retrieved file replaces the current file. Use /File Save to store a current file before you retrieve a new file.

To retrieve a worksheet file

1. Select /File Retrieve.

   If you haven't saved the current worksheet, you see a No/Yes prompt, asking whether you want to retrieve the file anyway. No returns you to the File menu; Yes displays the list of files in the current directory.

2. Select the file name you want to retrieve and press Enter.

/File Save

Purpose

Saves the current worksheet and settings.

To save a file

1. Select /File Save.

2. Enter the file name for the worksheet by using the default name, if a name appears; by using ← or → to highlight an existing name; by typing a new name; or by entering a new drive designation, path name, and file name. Press Enter.

3. If a file exists with the name you selected, select Backup, Cancel, or Replace.

   Selecting Replace replaces the existing file on disk with the active file you are saving. You cannot recover the replaced file. Use Backup to save a copy of the original file. Cancel ends the save procedure.

To save a file with a password

1. Select /File Save.
2. Type the file name, press the space bar, and type P. Press Enter.
3. Type a password of up to 15 characters (no spaces). A solid square appears for each letter. Memorize the upper- and lowercase letter combination. You must enter the exact password, which is case-sensitive when you next retrieve the file. Press Enter.
4. At the verify prompt, type the password again and press Enter. The file is saved.

/File Xtract

Purpose

Saves to disk a portion of the current worksheet as a separate worksheet.

Reminders: You can save the portion as it appears on the worksheet (with formulas) or save only the results of the formulas.

Extracted ranges that include formulas must include the cells to which the formulas refer, or the formulas are incorrect.

If CALC appears at the bottom of the screen, calculate the file by pressing F9 before extracting values.

To save to disk a portion of a file

1. Position the cursor at the upper left corner of the range you want to extract.
2. Select /File Xtract.
3. Select Formulas or Values.
4. At the prompt, type a file name other than the current file.
5. Specify the range of the file you want to extract as a separate file and press Enter.
6. If the name already exists, select Backup, Cancel, or Replace. The file is created on disk.

/Graph X/A/B/C/D/E/F

Purpose

Specifies the worksheet ranges that contain the data that you want to graph.

To specify the ranges that you want to graph

1. Select /Graph.
2. From the following options, select the ranges for x- or y-axis data or labels you want to enter:

Menu Item	Description
X	Enters an x-axis data range, which may be labels, such as *Jan*, *Feb*, *Mar*, and so on. This range may be used as labels for pie graph wedges and line, bar, and stacked-bar graphs.
A	Enters the first data range. **Note:** This item is the only data range used by a pie graph.

Menu Item	Description
B	Enters a second y-axis data range. Enters pie graph shading values and extraction values.
C	Enters a third data range.
D-F	Enters the fourth through the sixth data ranges.

3. Indicate the data range by entering the range address, using a range name, or highlighting the range.

4. Press Enter.

/Graph Group

Purpose

Selects the X and A through F data ranges for a graph at once, when data in adjacent rows and columns are in contiguous order.

To select a data range for a graph at once

1. Select /Graph Group.

2. Specify the range that contains X and A through F data values. The rows or columns must be adjacent and in the order X, A, B, C, D, E, and F.

3. Select Columnwise to graph the data ranges in columns or Rowwise to graph the data ranges in rows.

/Graph Name

Purpose

Stores graph settings for later use with the same worksheet.

Reminders: If you want to name a graph, make sure that the graph is the current graph before assigning a name.

You can use graphs in later work sessions only if you saved the graph settings by using /Graph Name Create, and then saved the worksheet with /File Save.

Note that /Graph Name Reset deletes all graph names in the current worksheet and all graph parameters.

To create or modify a graph name

1. Select /Graph Name.
2. Select Use, Create, Delete, Reset, or Table.

   Specify the graph name if you are switching to another graph, creating a new graph name, or deleting or resetting graph names.

   If you create a table of graph names, specify the location for the table.

/Graph Options Color/B&W

Purpose

Determines whether 1-2-3 displays graphs in color or black and white on the monitor, if you have color capability.

To set the color option
Select /Graph Options Color.

To set the black-and-white option
Select /Graph Options B&W.

Note
If you use a black-and-white printer, you can print graphs only in black and white, even if you saved the graphs with the color options set.

/Graph Options Data-Labels

Purpose
Labels graph points, using data contained in cells.

To assign data labels
1. Select /Graph Options Data-Labels.
2. Select the data range to which you want to assign labels. You can select from A-F, Group, and Quit.
3. Specify the range that contains the labels. Make this range the same size as the range you selected for A through F. If you group data ranges, the range selected must be the same size as all the data ranges combined.
4. From the following options, select the data label location, relative to the corresponding data points: Center, Left, Above, Right, and Below.

/Graph Options Format

Purpose
Selects the symbols and lines that identify and connect data points.

Some line and XY graphs present information more clearly if the data appears only as data points; other graphs present information better if the data is represented by a series of data points linked with a solid line. Use /Graph Options Format to select the kind of data points used for each data range (symbols, lines, or both).

To format graph options
1. Select /Graph Options Format.

2. Select from Graph or A through F to define the data ranges to format.

3. Select the data point type. You can choose from Lines, Symbols, Both, Neither, and Area.

/Graph Options Grid

Purpose
Overlays a grid on a graph to enhance readability.

To overlay a grid on a graph
1. Select /Graph Options Grid.

2. Select the type of grid. You can choose from Horizontal, Vertical, Both, and Clear. Only one choice is active at a time.

/Graph Options Legend

Purpose
Assigns labels that indicate which line, bar, or point belongs to a specific data range.

> **Reminder:** If, by using /Move, /Worksheet Insert, or /Worksheet Delete, you relocate a graph, 1-2-3 cannot adjust cell addresses used to create legends. Use range names to describe legend ranges.

To specify a graph legend

1. Select /Graph Options Legend.
2. Select from A through F or Range to assign a legend to a single data range or to all data ranges.
3. If you select from A through F, enter the text for the legend. If you select Range, specify the range that contains the legends.

Note

You also may specify a cell address or range name by preceding it with a backslash (\ ).

/Graph Options Scale

Purpose

Varies the scale along the y-axis. The x-axis scale can be varied on XY-type graphs.

> **Reminder:** Options within this command include:
>
> ▓ Making changes to the upper- or lower-axis end points.
>
> ▓ Choosing formats for numeric display. (Options are identical to formats in /Worksheet Global Format or /Range Format.)
>
> ▓ Improving the display of overlapping x-axis labels by skipping every specified occurrence, such as every second or third label.

To modify a graph scale
1. Select /Graph Options Scale.
2. Select from Y-Scale, X-Scale, and Skip.
3. If you select the Y-Scale or X-Scale menu items, select the menu item you want to scale. You can choose from Automatic, Manual, Lower, Upper, Format, Indicator, and Display.
4. If you select Skip, enter a number to indicate the frequency intervals at which the x-axis scale tick marks appear. Then press Enter.

Note
The Display option appears only if you select Y-Scale.

/Graph Options Titles

Purpose
Adds headings to the graph and to each axis.

To add titles to a graph
1. Select /Graph Options Titles.
2. Select First, Second, X-Axis, or Y-Axis to define the title you want to enter.
3. Enter a title, cell address, or range name of a cell that contains a title.

   To use cell contents for a title, type \ (backslash); then the cell address or range name, and press Enter.

/Graph Reset

Purpose
Cancels all or some of a graph's setting so that you can create a new graph or exclude one or more data ranges from the old graph.

To cancel graph settings

1. Select /Graph Reset.
2. Select from Graph, X, A through F, Ranges, or
   Options to clear or reset all current graph
   settings, specified data range(s), or graph
   options.

/Graph Save

Purpose

Saves graphs in a file and adds the PIC extension so
that you can print the graphs in PrintGraph (see
your Lotus documentation), Wysiwyg, or other
programs.

To save a graph

1. Select /Graph Save.
2. Specify a file name and press Enter. If you
   don't type an extension, 1-2-3 adds the PIC
   extension.

   If you type an existing file name, a Cancel or
   Replace prompt appears.

/Graph Type

Purpose

Selects from among the 1-2-3 graph types, according
to how you want to graph the data.

To select a graph type

1. Select /Graph Type.
2. Select a graph type from the options in the
   following list:

Menu Item	Description
Line	Graphs data ranges as lines.
Bar	Graphs data ranges as bars.
XY	Shows correlations between Y-axis data (A through F) and X-axis data; XY graphs have numeric data on both axes.
Stack-Bar	Displays how proportions change within the whole.
Pie	Displays how the whole is divided into component parts. Use only the A range to contain the values of each portion. Use the X range to label the pie wedges.
HLCO	Tracks items that vary over time. Commonly used in the stock market to show the price at which a stock opens and closes and the high and low prices throughout the day.
Mixed	Contains bar and line graphs. Relates trends in two distinct measurable quantities. Mixed graphs can contain up to three bars and three lines.
Features	Provides additional choices that enable you to control the appearance of the graph:
	Vertical orients the graph vertically (default selection).
	Horizontal rotates the graph so that the y-axis is horizontal and the x-axis is vertical.
	Stacked stacks ranges on top of each other.

Menu Item	Description
Features	Frame controls the adjustment of the graph frame, gutters, and zero lines.
	3D-Effect enhances bar, stack-bar, and mixed graphs by adding a three-dimensional look.

3. If you select Features Stacked or Features 3D-Effect, select Yes or No from the resulting menu.

   If you select Features Frame, select one or more options from the resulting menu to customize the appearance of the graph frame.

/Graph View

Purpose
Displays a graph on-screen.

Reminder: The system hardware and system configuration determine what appears on-screen.

To display a graph
1. Select /Graph View or F10 to display the current graph on-screen.
2. Press any key to return to the Graph menu.

/Move

Purpose

Moves ranges of labels, values, or formulas to different locations in the worksheet.

To move data

1. Select /Move.

   The Move what? prompt requests the range of the cells you want to move.

2. Highlight a range or type the range name or the range address and press Enter.

3. At the To where? prompt, enter the address of the upper left corner of the range to which the cells will be moved. Press Enter.

/Print [Printer, File, Encoded, Background]

Purpose

Prints worksheet contents.

/Print Printer prints directly to the printer. /Print File prints worksheet contents as an ASCII text file to disk so that you can import the file into other programs. /Print Encoded prints a print-image file to disk so that you may print the data later. /Print Background sends print output to an encoded file and then prints in the background.

> **Reminder:** When you select /Print Printer, /Print File, /Print Encoded, or /Print Background, the main print menu appears. All print settings apply equally to all four options. If you select /Print File and specify a range, for example, the next time you select /Print Printer (or /Print Encoded or /Print Background), 1-2-3 remembers the range you selected for /Print File.

To print a range

1. Select /Print Printer, /Print File, /Print Encoded, or /Print Background.

2. If you select /Print File, /Print Encoded, or /Print Background, enter the file name. If you select /Print File, 1-2-3 gives the file name a PRN extension automatically. If you select /Print Encoded or /Print Background, 1-2-3 gives the file name an ENC extension.

3. Select Range.

4. Specify the range you want to print; then select other options as needed.

5. Select Go to print the range.

Notes

To use /Print Background, you must load the BPRINT utility before starting 1-2-3.

If you didn't load BPRINT prior to loading 1-2-3, when you choose /Print Background, the computer beeps and an error message appears. Refer to the Lotus documentation for information on the BPRINT utility.

When you select /Print Background, a file with the extension ENC is created as you continue working. After the file is printed, 1-2-3 erases this file.

Throughout the following /Print commands, the individual Printer, File, Encoded, and Background

options appear in the headers as [P,F,E,B]. The
header /Print [P,F,E,B] Line, for example,
indicates that besides /Print Printer Line, you can
select /Print File Line, /Print Encoded Line, or /Print
Background Line.

/Print [P,F,E,B] Align

Purpose

Aligns 1-2-3's internal line counter to the top of a
physical page in the printer, and resets the page
number to 1.

Reminder: Use this command only when the
paper is at the top of a new page.

To synchronize 1-2-3 with the printer

If necessary, position the printer paper so that the
top of a page is aligned with the print head. Select
/Print [P,F,E,B] Align to synchronize 1-2-3 with the
printer.

/Print [P,F,E,B] Clear

Purpose

Clears some or all print settings and options and
returns them to their default settings.

Reminders: This option is the only way to clear
borders after they are set.

Print parameters remain in effect until you issue
different instructions. To issue a new set of parameters, use /Print [P,F,E,B] Clear.

To clear print settings

Select /Print [P,F,E,B] Clear. Then select All, Range, Borders, or Format.

/Print [P,F,E,B] Go

Purpose

Sends data to a printer or file.

To send data to a printer or file

1. Select /Print Printer, /Print File, /Print Encoded, or /Print Background.
2. For /Print File or /Print Encoded, enter the print file name. With /Print File, 1-2-3 gives the file name a default PRN extension. With /Print Encoded, 1-2-3 gives the file name an END extension. For /Print Background, specify the name of the encoded file.
3. Select Range.
4. Specify the range to be printed. Then select other options as needed.
5. Select Go to print the range.

/Print [P,F,E,B] Line

Purpose

Advances printer paper by one line.

To advance the printer page by one line

1. Select /Print [P,F,E,B].
2. Select Line to advance the paper by one line.

   Repeat the keystroke (or, select Line) as often as needed to advance the paper.

/Print [P,F,E,B] Options Borders

Purpose

Prints on every page the rows and/or columns you select from the worksheet.

Reminder: If you include in the print range the rows and/or columns specified as borders, they print twice.

To print rows or columns on every page

1. Select /Print [P,F,E,B] Options Borders.
2. Select Columns or Rows.
3. Specify the borders range and press Enter.

Note

The only way to remove borders which already are set is by selecting /Print [P,F,E,B] Clear Borders.

/Print [P,F,E,B] Options Footer/Header

Purpose

Prints a footer above the bottom margin or a header below the top margin of each page.

To print a footer or header

1. Select /Print [P,F,E,B] Options.
2. Select Footer or Header. You can type a footer or header as wide as the margin and paper width (up to 240 characters).
3. Press Enter.

Notes

You can use headers and footers for titles, dates, and page numbers.

To print the date and page number by default in the footer or header, type @ (at sign) where you want the date to appear and type # (number sign) where you want the page number to appear.

To enter the contents of a cell into a header or footer, type \ (backslash) followed by the cell address.

To separate the footer or header into as many as three segments, type | (vertical bar) where you want a segment to end and a new segment to begin. To print a header or a footer in three segments with a system date of July 25, 1992, at page 21, type the following line:

@|Hill and Dale|Page #

This data prints as:

25-Jul-92   Hill and Dale Page 21

To center one data segment, type | (vertical bar) to the left of the data. To left-justify the data, include no vertical bars. To right-justify the data, insert two vertical bars before the data you want to justify. To right-justify the page number, for example, type ||Page #.

/Print [P,F,E,B] Options Margins

Purpose

Changes the left, right, top, and bottom margins.

To set margins for printing

1. Select /Print [P,F,E,B] Options Margins.

2. Select Left, Right, Top, Bottom, or None to
   specify the margins.

3. If you selected Left, Right, Top, or Bottom,
   enter the margin size (in inches) and press
   Enter.

/Print [P,F,E,B] Options Other

Purpose
Selects the form and formatting in which cells print.

To select the format in which cells print
1. Select /Print [P,F,E,B] Options Other.

2. To specify a printing method, select As-
   Displayed, Cell-Formulas, Formatted, or
   Unformatted.

/Print [P,F,E,B] Options Pg-Length

Purpose
Specifies the number of lines per page, using a
standard 6-lines-per-inch page height.

To specify the number of lines per page
1. Select /Print [P,F,E,B] Options Pg-Length.

2. Enter the number of lines per page if that number is different from the number that appears.

   You can specify a page length of 1 to 100 lines.

3. Press Enter.

/Print [P,F,E,B] Options Setup

Purpose
Sends formatting commands to the printer.

> **Reminders:** Don't combine setup strings with the menu commands for the same feature. The result is unpredictable.
>
> Refer to the printer manual for a list of printer control codes or escape codes.

To send formatting codes to the printer
1. Select /Print [P,F,E,B] Options Setup.
2. Enter the setup string.

   If a setup string was already entered, press Esc to clear the string. Each control code within the setup string must begin with a backslash (\) and upper- or lowercase letters must be typed as shown in the printer manual.
3. Press Enter.

Note
1-2-3 setup strings usually are three-digit numbers, preceded by a backslash (\). The EPSON printer control code for condensed print, for example, is 15. Therefore, the 1-2-3 setup string is \015.

/Print [P,F,E,B] Page

Purpose
Controls paper feed by moving the paper to the bottom of the page for printing any footer, and then

by advancing the paper until the print head is at the top of the next page.

To control paper feed

1. Select /Print [P,F,E,B].

2. Select Page to print any footer at the bottom of the page, and to position the print head at the top of the next page.

/Print [P,F,E,B] Range

Purpose

Defines the area of the worksheet you want to print.

To define the area you want to print

1. Select /Print [P,F,E,B] Range.

2. To specify the range to print, type the range address, highlight the range, or enter an assigned range name.

3. Press Enter.

/Quit

Purpose

Exits 1-2-3 and returns to the operating system.

Reminder: All files not saved with /File Save are lost when you exit 1-2-3.

To exit 1-2-3

1. Select /Quit.

2. To quit 1-2-3 and return to the operating system, select Yes; to return to 1-2-3 and the current worksheet, select No.

If you altered the current worksheet without saving these changes, another Yes/No prompt appears.

3. Select Yes to quit without saving (abandon the changes) if you made changes to the worksheet. Select No to return to the worksheet.

Notes

If you start 1-2-3 from the Access System menu, you return to this menu when you quit 1-2-3. Select Exit from the Access System menu to leave this menu and return to the operating system.

If you type 123 to exit 1-2-3, you return to the operating system when you quit.

/Range Erase

Purpose

Erases the contents of a single cell or a range of cells, but retains the format of the cell or range of cells.

To erase the contents of a range

1. Select /Range Erase.

2. Specify the range you want to erase by highlighting the range or typing the cell address or range name, and press Enter.

/Range Format

Purpose

Specifies how cells are to display data.

Reminders: /Range formats take precedence over /Worksheet Global formats.

/Range Format rounds only the appearance of the displayed number, not the number used for calculation. Therefore, displayed or printed numbers can appear to be incorrect answers to formulas. Use @ROUND to ensure that the values in calculations are rounded properly.

To format a range

1. Select /Range Format.
2. Select a format from the following menu items:

Menu Item	Description
Fixed	Sets the number of decimal places that appear on-screen.
Sci	Displays numbers, using scientific notation.
Currency	Displays currency symbols, such as $, and commas.
,	Inserts commas to mark thousands and multiples of thousands.
General	Displays values in standard format.
+/−	Represents values in a horizontal bar graph format. Positive numbers appear as plus (+) symbols; negative numbers appear as minus (−) symbols.
Percent	Displays a decimal number as a whole percentage by multiplying the number by 100 and using % (percent symbol).

Menu Item	Description
Date	Displays serial-date numbers in several formats. To choose a format, select a number from one of the following options:

1	DD-MMM-YY	12-Jan-92
2	DD-MMM	12-Jan
3	MMM-YY	Jan-92
4	(Long Intn'l)	01/12/92
5	(Short Intn'l)	01/12

Menu Item	Description
Time	Displays time fractions.
Text	Continues to evaluate formulas as numbers but formulas appear on-screen as text.
Hidden	Hides contents from displaying on-screen and doesn't print them but still evaluates contents.
Reset	Returns the format to current /Worksheet Global format.

3. If prompted, enter the number of decimal places you want to appear. The full value of a cell is used for calculation, not the value that appears on-screen.

4. At the prompt, enter the range address, highlight the range, or use an assigned range name to specify the range.

5. Press Enter. The data appears formatted on-screen.

/Range Input

Purpose

Enables cell-pointer movement in unprotected cells only.

Reminders: To use /Range Input effectively, organize the worksheet so that the data-entry cells are together.

Before you use /Range Input, use /Range Unprot to identify unprotected data entry cells. You don't have to enable /Worksheet Global Protection to use /Range Input.

To restrict cell-pointer movement to unprotected cells

1. Select /Range Input.
2. Specify the input range. Include a range that covers all cells in which you want to display or enter data.
3. Press Enter. The upper left corner of the input range moves to the upper left corner of the screen. Cell-pointer movement is restricted to unprotected cells in the designated input range.
4. You now can enter data only in the unprotected cells. Press Esc or Enter to exit /Range Input.

/Range Justify

Purpose

Fits text within a desired range by wrapping words to form complete paragraphs and redistributes words so that text lines are approximately the same length.

To justify text

1. Select /Range Justify.

2. Highlight the range in which you want to justify text. Highlight only the first row of the text column to enable 1-2-3 to use additional rows to justify text as needed.

3. Press Enter to justify the text.

/Range Label

Purpose

Selects how you want to align text labels in the cells.

To align text labels

1. Select /Range Label.

2. Select Left, Right, or Center.

3. At the prompt, enter the range address, highlight the range, or use an assigned range name to specify the range. Press Enter.

/Range Name

Purpose

Assigns a name to a cell or a range of cells.

> **Reminder:** Moving one or more corners of a range can redefine the range name. Check the addresses to which a range name applies by issuing /Range Name Create and selecting the name in question. The address of the selected range name appears on-screen.

Note

Rather than using cell addresses, use range names to make formulas and macros easy to read and understand.

To create a range name

1. Select /Range Name Create.

2. At the prompt, type a range name (the range name can contain a maximum of 15 characters). Avoid symbols other than the underline and backslash. Also avoid using names similar to cell addresses (such as P1). Press Enter.

3. At the prompt, specify the range you want to name and press Enter.

To create range names from worksheet labels

1. Select /Range Name Labels.

2. Select Right, Down, Left, or Up.

3. At the prompt, specify the range of labels to use as range names for adjacent cells by entering the range address or highlighting the range. Press Enter.

To delete one or more range names

1. Select /Range Name.

2. Select Delete to delete a single range name. Select Reset to delete all range names.

   If you select Delete, type or highlight the name you want to delete and press Enter. Formulas that contain the range names will now use cell and range addresses.

To create a table of existing range names and addresses

Select /Range Name Table and press Enter. The table appears.

Notes

Use a range name when you enter an @function. Rather than entering an @function as

@SUM(D3..D24), for example, type the function as
@SUM(EXPENSES), if you gave the range D3..D24 the
name *Expenses*.

Use a range name when you respond to a prompt.
When the program requests a print range, for
example, provide a range name, as in the following
example:

Enter print range: JULREPORT.

/Range Prot/Unprot

Purpose
Changes the protection status of a range.

To unprotect a cell or a range of cells
1. Select /Range Unprot.
2. Specify the range and press Enter.

To remove the unprotected status from a range
1. Select /Range Prot.
2. Specify the range and press Enter.

Notes
/Range Prot and /Range Unprot affect data entry
only when /Worksheet Global Protection is enabled.

On some monitors, the display of the contents of
unprotected cells increases in intensity or changes
color.

Use /Range Prot, /Range Unprot, and /Worksheet
Global Protection to protect worksheets from
accidental changes. /Range Unprot identifies the cell
contents you can change when /Worksheet Global
Protection is used, and also is used with the /Range
Input command.

/Range Search

Purpose

Finds or replaces text within a range. You can limit searches and replaces to labels or formulas.

Reminder: Although you can find or replace numbers in formulas, you cannot use /Range Search to find or replace numbers.

To find or replace text

1. Select /Range Search.
2. Specify the range you want to search.
3. At the prompt, enter the text string to find or replace. You can use upper- or lowercase text.
4. Select Formulas, Labels, or Both.
5. Select Find or Replace.
6. Depending on your choice in step 5, take one of the following actions:

    If you select Find, 1-2-3 finds and displays (in the control panel) the cell that contains the specified text. Select Next to find other occurrences or Quit to stop the search.

    If you select Replace, type the replacement string and press Enter. 1-2-3 finds and displays the cell in the control panel that contains the specified text. The specified text is highlighted. Then choose Replace, All, Next, or Quit.

    Replace replaces the string and moves on to the next *occurrence*. All replaces all occurrences of the text and returns you to READY mode. Next moves on to the next occurrence without changes. 1-2-3 Quit stops the search.

/Range Trans

Purpose

Copies data from one location and orientation to another location and orientation. Formulas are converted to values.

> **Reminder:** Make sure that the file is calculated. If CALC appears at the bottom of the screen, press F9 to recalculate the file.

To transpose data

1. Select /Range Trans.
2. Specify the range you want to transpose and press Enter.
3. Specify the upper left corner of the area where you want the transposed data to appear.
4. Press Enter. The data transposes immediately.

/Range Value

Purpose

Replaces formulas in the same or new location with their resulting values.

Copies labels and string formulas and converts string (text) formulas to labels.

> **Reminder:** Make sure that the file is calculated. If CALC appears at the bottom of the screen, press F9 to recalculate the file.

To replace formulas with values

1. Select /Range Value.
2. At the Convert what? prompt, specify the source range and press Enter.
3. At the To where? prompt, specify the upper left corner cell of the destination range and press Enter.

   The values appear in the destination range. These values preserve the numeric formats used in the original formulas.

/System

Purpose

Exits 1-2-3 temporarily so that you can run DOS commands or other programs. To return to 1-2-3 and the worksheet in which you were working, type EXIT.

> **Reminder:** Be sure that the programs you run from 1-2-3 fit in the computer's available memory. Don't load or run memory-resident programs after you select /System.

Note

Prior to using /System, save all work.

To exit 1-2-3 temporarily

1. Select /System.
2. Type the DOS commands or programs.
3. When you finish running a program, return to DOS.
4. To return to 1-2-3 from the DOS prompt, type EXIT and press Enter.

/Worksheet Column

Purpose

Adjusts the column width of one or more columns.

To adjust column width

1. Select /Worksheet Column.

2. Select Set-Width, Reset-Width, Hide, Display, or Column-Range.

3. Depending on your choice in step 2, take one of the following actions:

   If you select Set-Width, enter the new column width by typing the number of characters, or by pressing ← or → to shrink or expand the column.

   If you select Hide or Display, indicate which columns you want to change.

   If you select Column-Range, select Set-Width or Reset-Width, indicate the columns you want to change, enter the column width as a number, or press ← or → to shrink or expand the column(s). Press Enter.

/Worksheet Delete

Purpose

Deletes one or more columns or rows in the worksheet.

To delete columns or rows

1. Select /Worksheet Delete.

2. Select Column or Row.

3. At the prompt, specify a range that contains the columns or rows you want to delete and press Enter.

Note

Entire rows and columns are deleted all the way to the edges of the worksheet.

/Worksheet Erase

Purpose

Erases the entire worksheet and resets all cell formats, label prefixes, and command settings to the original values.

> **Reminder:** Be sure that you save the active file before using /Worksheet Erase.

To erase the current worksheet from memory

1. Select /Worksheet Erase, then select Yes or No.

2. Select Yes to erase the current worksheet from memory or No to return to READY mode.

Note

If you made changes to the worksheet and didn't save the file, you see a Yes/No prompt. Select Yes to erase the worksheet or No to return to READY mode so that you can save the current worksheet.

/Worksheet Global Column-Width

Purpose

Sets column width for the entire worksheet.

To set the global worksheet column width

1. Select /Worksheet Global Column-Width.

2. At the prompt, enter a number for the column width used most frequently, or press → to increase column width or ← to decrease column width.

3. Press Enter.

/Worksheet Global Default

Purpose

Specifies display formats and start-up settings for hardware.

Used to control how 1-2-3 works with the printer, the disk and directory accessed by default, which international displays are used, and which kind of clock appears.

To specify worksheet default settings

1. Select /Worksheet Global Default.

2. Select the setting you want to change:

Menu Item	Description
Printer	Specifies printer settings and connections. You can choose from the following options:
	Interface selects parallel or serial port.
	AutoLF instructs 1-2-3 to insert a line feed by default after each printer line.
	Left specifies the left margin. The default is 4. You can choose from a range of 0 to 240 text characters.

continues

Menu Item	Description
	Right specifies the right margin. The default is 76. You can choose from a range of 0 to 240.
	Top specifies the top margin. The default is 2. You can choose from a range of 0 to 32 text characters.
	Bottom specifies the bottom margin. The default is 2. You can choose from a range of 0 to 32.
	Pg-Length specifies page length. The default is 66 lines per page. You can choose from 1 to 100 lines per page.
	Wait pauses for a page insert at the end of each page.
	Setup sets the default setup string to be used when printing.
	Name enables you to select from multiple printers, if you installed these printers during the Install procedure.
	Delay specifies the number of minutes to wait before generating a printer error.
Directory	Specifies the directory for read or write operations. Press Esc to clear the current entry, type the new directory, and press Enter.
Status	Displays settings for /Worksheet Global Default.

Menu Item	Description
Update	Saves to disk the current global defaults for use with the next startup.
Other	Enables you to choose from the following options:
	International specifies display settings for Punctuation, Currency, Date, Time, and Negative formats.
	Help enables you to choose from Instant or Removable.
	Clock specifies how the date and time indicator in the lower left corner of the screen appears. Clock is chosen if you previously chose None to restore the display of the date and time indicator. Filename displays current file name.
	Undo enables or disables the Undo feature.
	Beep turns on or off the computer's sound.
	Add-In specifies an add-in program to be attached each time you start 1-2-3.
	Expanded-Memory controls how 1-2-3 uses expanded memory. Standard (the default) maximizes speed; Enhanced allows larger worksheets (space is required on disk).
Autoexec	Enables or disables the capability to run autoexecute macros.

/Worksheet Global Format

Purpose

Defines the default display format for numeric values and formulas in the worksheet.

To define the default numeric format

1. Select /Worksheet Global Format.

2. Select Fixed, Sci, Currency, , (comma), General, +/–, Percent, Date, Text, or Hidden. Refer to /Range Format for explanations of these choices.

3. After you select Fixed, Sci, Currency, , (comma), or Percent, enter the number of decimal places at the prompt, and then press Enter.

Note

Numbers stored in the cells are accurate up to 15 digits to the right of the decimal. The stored numbers—not the numbers that appear on-screen—are used in calculations.

/Worksheet Global Label-Prefix

Purpose

Selects text label alignment throughout the worksheet.

To align label text globally

1. Select /Worksheet Global Label-Prefix.

2. Select Left, Right, or Center.

/Worksheet Global Protection

Purpose
Protects the worksheet or file from being changed.

Reminders: Cells marked with /Range Unprot are unprotected when worksheet protection is on.

Before or after you protect the entire worksheet, you can use /Range Unprot to specify cells that you want to modify.

To protect a worksheet
1. Select /Worksheet Global Protection.
2. Select one of the following options:

Menu Item	Description
Enable	Protects the worksheet. Only cells specified with /Range Unprot can be modified.
Disable	Removes protection from the worksheet, and then any cell can be modified.

/Worksheet Global Recalculation

Purpose
Defines how a file recalculates and how many times the file calculates.

To define worksheet recalculation
1. Select /Worksheet Global Recalculation.
2. Select one of the following options:

Menu Item	Description
Natural	Before recalculating a given formula, recalculates all other formulas upon which the formula depends.
Columnwise	Starts at the top of column A and recalculates downward, then moves to column B and recalculates downward, and so on.
Rowwise	Starts at the beginning of row 1 and recalculates to the end of the row, then continues through proceeding rows.
Automatic	Recalculates after you modify cell contents.
Manual	Recalculates only when you press F9 (Calc) or when {CALC} is encountered in a macro. The CALC indicator appears at the bottom of the screen when recalculation is needed.
Iteration	Recalculates the worksheet a specified number of times.

3. If you select Iteration, enter a number from 1 to 50 at the prompt. The default setting is 1. Iteration works with Columnwise and Rowwise recalculations or with Natural recalculation when the worksheet contains a circular reference.

4. If you select Columnwise or Rowwise recalculation, you might need to repeat step 1 and select Iteration in step 2. In step 3, enter the number of recalculations necessary for correct results.

Columnwise and Rowwise recalculations often require multiple calculations to ensure that all worksheet results are correct.

/Worksheet Global Zero

Purpose
Suppresses zeros from appearing in the worksheet, on-screen, and in printed reports or displays a label.

To suppress the display of zeros
1. Select /Worksheet Global Zero.
2. You can choose from the following commands:

Menu Item	Description
No	Displays cells that contain zero, or a result of zero, as zero.
Yes	Suppresses the display of cells that contain zero or a result of zero.
Label	Displays a label that you enter in place of zero or in place of zero as a result.

3. If you select Label, at the prompt enter the label you want to display and press Enter.

Note
Precede the label with an apostrophe (') for left alignment or a caret (^) for center alignment. Default label alignment is set at right alignment.

/Worksheet Insert

Purpose

Inserts one or more blank columns or rows in the worksheet. Use this command to add space for formulas, data, or text.

To insert columns or rows

1. Select /Worksheet Insert.
2. Select Column or Row.
3. Depending on your choice in step 2, take one of the following actions:

   If you select Column, highlight one cell for each column you want to insert.

   If you select Row, highlight one cell for each row you want to insert.
4. Press Enter.

/Worksheet Learn

Purpose

Specifies a worksheet range (the "learn range") in which to record keystrokes when you type them.

To specify a range in which to record keystrokes

1. Select /Worksheet Learn Range.
2. Highlight the column range and press Enter.
3. To begin recording keystrokes, press Alt-F5 (Learn).

   Enter all keystrokes, and press Alt-F5 to turn off the recording.
4. Go to the learn range and edit the macro keystrokes if necessary.

5. Assign a name to the macro by using /Range Name Create.

To clear or cancel a learn range

1. Select /Worksheet Learn.

2. Select Cancel to cancel an existing learn range without erasing any keystrokes in the learn range.

   Select Erase to clear all the keystrokes presently recorded in the learn range.

Notes

Make sure that you define a learn range large enough to accommodate the macro instructions. If you don't, 1-2-3 turns off the learn range when the defined area is filled.

Recording keystrokes saves you from having to write down or memorize the keystrokes for macros.

All mouse actions and some special keys aren't recorded by 1-2-3 in the learn range. Learn records Help (F1) but doesn't record any keystrokes entered while using Help.

/Worksheet Page

Purpose

Manually inserts page breaks in printed worksheets.

To insert page breaks

1. Move the cell pointer to where you want the page break.

2. Select /Worksheet Page. A row is inserted and a double colon (::) appears in the left column.

/Worksheet Status

Purpose

Displays some global worksheet settings and memory information.

To display the worksheet status

1. Select /Worksheet Status.

   The status of the worksheet appears on-screen.

2. Press any key to return to the worksheet.

/Worksheet Titles

Purpose

Displays column or row headings that might otherwise scroll off-screen in worksheet that contains data that cannot display on one screen.

To freeze titles on-screen

1. To place column headings at the top of the screen, move the cell pointer so that the column headings you want to freeze on-screen occupy the top rows of the worksheet.

   If you want row headings along the extreme left edge of the screen, move the cell pointer so that the columns that contain the extreme left-row headings are at the left edge of the screen.

2. Move the cell pointer one row below the lowest row you want to use as a title and one column to the right of the rightmost column you want to use as title(s).

3. Select /Worksheet Titles.

4. Select one of the following options:

Horizontal freezes the rows above the cell pointer.

Vertical freezes the columns to the left of the cell pointer.

Both freezes the rows above and the columns to the left of the cell pointer.

Clear unfreezes all the rows and columns.

/Worksheet Window

Purpose

Displays two parts of a worksheet at the same time.

You can split the worksheet horizontally or vertically. The two parts of the worksheet can scroll separately or together and follow the same cell-pointer movements.

To display a worksheet window

1. Select /Worksheet Window.
2. Select one of the following options:

Menu Item	Description
Horizontal	Splits the worksheet into two horizontal windows at the cell pointer.
Vertical	Splits the worksheet into two vertical windows at the cell pointer.
Sync	Synchronizes two windows so that they scroll together.
Unsync	Enables you to scroll two windows independently of each other.
Clear	Removes the right or bottom window.

Note

Press F6 to move the cell pointer between windows.

WYSIWYG COMMAND REFERENCE

1-2-3 Releases 2.3 and 2.4 provide you with the tools you need to present worksheets in an attractive format. This section provides an alphabetical listing of all the Wysiwyg commands available when you press colon (:). Before you can use Wysiwyg commands, you must load the add-in in memory.

Note

If you installed Wysiwyg with the 1-2-3 Release 2.4 program—the default choice—Wysiwyg loads into memory each time you start 1-2-3.

To load the add-in in memory

1. Select /Add-In Attach.
2. From the list of add-ins that appears, highlight WYSIWYG.ADN and press Enter.
3. Select No-Key.
4. To return to the 1-2-3 worksheet, select Quit.

:Display Colors

Purpose

Specifies worksheet colors for background, text, data in unprotected cells, cell pointer, grid, worksheet frame, negative values, lines, and drop shadows. Also modifies the hue of the eight colors that 1-2-3 uses with Wysiwyg.

Reminder: :Display Colors is the only :Display command that affects the worksheets or graphics you print and only affects worksheets and graphics if you have a color printer.

only if you have a color printer

To display colors

1. Select :Display Colors.

2. Select one of the following options:

Menu Item	Description
Background	Sets the worksheet background color.
Text	Sets the color of worksheet text, numbers, and formulas.
Unprot	Sets the color of data in unprotected cells.
Cell-Pointer	Sets the color of the cell pointer.
Grid	Sets the color of the worksheet grid lines that you display on-screen using :Display Options Grid Yes.
Frame	Sets the color of the worksheet frame.
Neg	Sets the color of negative values.
Lines	Sets the color of lines you add to the worksheet using :Format Lines.
Shadow	Sets the color of drop shadows that you add to the worksheet using :Format Lines Shadow Set.

continues

Menu Item	Description
Replace	Modifies the hue of the eight Wysiwyg colors. Choose a color, then type a color value from 0 to 63.

3. If you select an option other than Replace, you can select Black, White, Red, Green, Dark-Blue, Cyan, Yellow, or Magenta.

Note
To update Wysiwyg to use the new color settings in future sessions, select :Display Default Update.

:Display Default

Purpose
Creates a new set of default display settings. Also replaces current display settings with default display settings.

Reminder: The default display settings are stored in the Wysiwyg configuration file WYSIWYG.CNF. 1-2-3 uses this file whenever you load Wysiwyg in memory.

To change the display default settings
1. Select :Display Default.
2. Select Restore to replace the current display settings with the default display settings.

   Select Update to save the current display settings as the default display settings.

:Display Font-Directory

Purpose

Specifies the directory where 1-2-3 looks for the fonts needed for the screen display and for printing.

> **Reminder:** If you select a directory that doesn't contain font files, 1-2-3 displays and prints in the system font (Courier).

To specify the font directory

1. Select :Display Font-Directory.
2. Press Esc to delete the current directory setting.
3. Type the drive letter and path name of the new directory. Press Enter.

Notes

The default font directory is the WYSIWYG subdirectory of the 1-2-3 Release 2.3 or 2.4 program directory; for example, C:\123R24\WYSIWYG>.

To update Wysiwyg to use the new font directory settings in future sessions, select :Display Default Update.

:Display Mode

Purpose

Changes between graphics and text display modes, and between black-and-white and color.

> **Reminder:** Graphics display mode is the Wysiwyg default mode. Color and black-and-white work only in graphics display mode.

To modify the display mode
1. Select :Display Mode.
2. Select one of the following options:

Menu Item	Description
Graphics	Sets the worksheet display so that it appears similar to the final printed output.
Text	Sets the worksheet display to appear as the standard 1-2-3 display (without Wysiwyg loaded).
B&W	Sets worksheet display to black-and-white (monochrome).
Color	Sets worksheet display to color.

Note
To update Wysiwyg to use the new display mode settings in future sessions, select :Display Default Update.

:Display Options

Purpose
Affects the display of the worksheet frame, grid lines, page breaks, and the cell pointer. Also affects brightness and enables you to select a graphics display adapter.

To modify the display options

1. Select :Display Options.

2. Select one of the following options:

Menu Item	Description
Frame	Changes the appearance of or hides the worksheet frame. You can select from the following frame settings:

1-2-3 displays the standard worksheet frame.

Enhanced (the default) displays a worksheet frame with lines separating the column letters and row numbers in the frame.

Relief displays a sculpted worksheet frame, replaces the cyan color with gray, and turns brightness to high.

Special replaces the column letters and row numbers of the worksheet frame with horizontal and vertical rulers in the following way:

Characters displays rulers in 10-point characters with 6 lines per inch; Inches displays rulers in inches; Metric displays rulers in centimeters; Points/Picas displays rulers in points and picas.

None hides the worksheet frame. |
| Grid | Yes turns on the worksheet grid lines; No turns off the grid lines. |

continues

Menu Item	Description
Page-Breaks	Yes displays Wysiwyg page-break symbols; No hides them.
Cell-Pointer	Solid displays the cell pointer as a solid-colored rectangle. Outline displays the cell pointer as a rectangular border around the current cell or range.
Intensity	Normal displays the on-screen appearance at normal intensity. High displays the on-screen appearance at high intensity.
Adapter	Enables you to specify the graphics display adapter to use. Auto is the default.

Notes

To insert page breaks, set a print range with :Print Range Set, and then use :Worksheet Page.

To update Wysiwyg to use the new options settings in future sessions, select :Display Default Update.

:Display Rows

Purpose

Specifies the number of rows that 1-2-3 displays on-screen while in graphics mode.

Reminder: 1-2-3 might display fewer or more rows than you specify; the number depends on the size of the default font and the graphics adapter card.

To choose the number of rows that appear on-screen

1. Select :Display Rows.
2. Type a number from 16 to 60.
3. Press Enter.

Notes

1-2-3 can display from 16 to 60 rows. The default number depends on the display mode you selected during installation.

To update Wysiwyg so that it uses the new rows setting in future sessions, select :Display Default Update.

:Display Zoom

Purpose

Enlarges or reduces the size of worksheet cells and affects the number of rows and columns the screen displays.

To enlarge or reduce the size of worksheet cells

1. Select :Display Zoom.
2. Select one of the following options:

Menu Item	Description
Tiny	Reduces cells to 63 percent of normal size.
Small	Reduces cells to 87 percent of normal size.
Normal	Displays cells at normal size (100 percent).
Large	Enlarges cells to 125 percent of normal size.

continues

Menu Item	Description
Huge	Enlarges cells to 150 percent of normal size.
Manual	Reduces or enlarges cells from 25 to 400 percent of their normal size. Type a number from 25 to 400 and press Enter.

Note

To update Wysiwyg to use the new zoom setting in future sessions, select :Display Default Update.

:Format Bold

Purpose

Changes data in a cell or range from normal to bold or vice versa.

To boldface data

1. Select :Format Bold.

2. Select Set to add bold to data in a cell or range, or select Clear to remove bold from data in a cell or range.

3. At the prompt, specify the cell or range and then press Enter.

:Format Color

Purpose

Displays and prints cell or ranges in seven colors.

(NEED COLOR PRINTER)

> **Reminder:** You need a color monitor to display colors and a color printer to print colors.

To select color text

1. Select :Format Color.
2. Select one of the following options:

Menu Item	Description
Text	Changes the color of text in a cell or range. You can choose Normal, Red, Green, Dark-Blue, Cyan, Yellow, or Magenta.
Background	Changes the color of the background of a cell or range. You can choose Normal, Red, Green, Dark-Blue, Cyan, Yellow, or Magenta.
Negative	Assigns a color for negative values in a range. You can choose Normal or Red.
Reverse	Switches the background and text colors in a cell or range.

3. At the prompt, specify the cell or range and then press Enter.

Notes

Normal returns the color of the range to the color you set with :Display Colors.

To display negative values in a color other than red, use :Display Colors Negative.

:Format Font

Purpose

Changes the font of a cell or range, specifies the default font for a file, replaces fonts in the current font set, updates and restores the default font set, and saves font libraries in files on disk.

> **Reminder:** You can use up to eight fonts in any file.

To select fonts

1. Select :Format Font.
2. Select one of the following options:

Menu Item	Description
1 to 8	Changes the font of a cell or range to the numbered font after you specify the range.
Replace	Replaces one of the eight fonts in the current font set. Select from 1 through 8 to select the font you want to replace. After selecting a number, you can choose from Swiss, Dutch, Courier, XSymbol, and Other. Other enables you to pick a list of typefaces from a list of extended typefaces. Enter a number from 3 to 72 to select a point size.
Default	Restore replaces the current font set with the default font set. Update creates a new default font set.

Menu Item	Description
Library	Retrieve loads the font set you specify from the fonts that you saved on disk previously. Save stores the current font set in a font library file on disk under the name you specify. Erase deletes from disk the font library file you specify.

Notes

When you select :Format Font, fonts 1 through 8 comprise the current on-screen font set.

Unless you enter a different extension, 1-2-3 adds the extension AFS to font libraries.

:Format Italics

Purpose

Changes data in a cell or range from standard to italics or vice versa.

To italicize data

1. Select :Format Italics.

2. Select Set to add italics to data in a cell or range or Clear to remove italics from data in a cell or range.

3. Specify the cell or range and then press Enter.

*AROUND A CELL
OR RANGE OF CElls.*

:Format Lines

Purpose

Draws or clears single, double, or wide lines along the left, right, top, and bottom edges of cells or ranges, and adds (or removes) a drop shadow to cells or ranges.

To add lines to a worksheet

1. Select :Format Lines.

2. Select one of the following options:

Menu Item	Description
Outline	Draws a single line around the edges of a cell or range.
Left	Draws a single line along the left edge of a cell or range.
Right	Draws a single line along the right edge of a cell or range.
Top	Draws a single line along the top edge of a cell or range.
Bottom	Draws a single line along the bottom edge of a cell or range.
All	Draws a single line around the edges of all cells in a range.
Double	Draws a double line where you specify. You can select from Outline, Left, Right, Top, Bottom, or All.
Wide	Draws a thick line where you specify. You can select from Outline, Left, Right, Top, Bottom, or All.

Menu Item	Description
Clear	Removes lines from a cell or range you specify. You can select from Outline, Left, Right, Top, Bottom, or All.
Shadow	Set adds a drop shadow to a cell or range. Clear removes a drop shadow from a cell or range of cells.

3. At the prompt, specify the cell or range and then press Enter.

:Format Reset

Purpose

Removes all formatting from a cell or range, and returns font and color settings to the defaults that were set with the :Display commands.

To remove Wysiwyg formatting

1. Select :Format Reset.
2. At the prompt, specify the cell or range and then press Enter.

Note

:Format Reset doesn't affect formats set with /Range Format, /Worksheet Global Format, or the Wysiwyg formatting sequences.

:Format Shade

Purpose

Adds or removes light, dark, or solid shading to a cell or range.

> **Reminder:** Solid shading hides the data in a cell or range unless you use :Format Color Text to select another color for the data.

To add shading

1. Select :Format Shade.
2. Select one of the following options:

Menu Item	Description
Light	Adds light shading to a cell or range.
Dark	Adds dark shading to a cell or range.
Solid	Adds solid shading to a cell or range.
Clear	Removes shading from a cell or range.

3. Specify the cell or range and then press Enter.

Note

Solid shading prints in black, even if you have a color printer.

:Format Underline

Purpose

Adds a single, double, or wide underline to a cell or range. Also removes underlining.

Reminder: Underlining appears only under data and doesn't appear in blank cells or blank parts of a cell.

To add underlining

1. Select :Format Underline.
2. Select one of the following options:

Menu Item	Description
Single	Adds a single underline to a cell range.
Double	Adds a double underline to a cell range.
Wide	Adds a thick underline to a cell range.
Clear	Removes underlining from a cell range.

3. Specify the cell or range and then press Enter.

Notes

Underlining is the same color you selected with :Display Colors Text.

Use :Format Lines to underline entire cells, or blank cells.

:Graph Add

Purpose

Adds a graphic to a worksheet.

To add a graphic

1. Select **:G**raph **A**dd.
2. Choose one of the following options:

Menu Item	Description
Current	Adds the current graph to the worksheet when you specify the range in which you want the graphic to appear.
Named	Adds a named graph from the current file to the worksheet when you specify a named graph from the current file, and then specify the range in which you want the graph to appear.
PIC	Adds a 1-2-3 graph saved in a PIC file to the worksheet when you specify a graph file with a PIC extension, and then specify the range in which you want the graph to appear.
Metafile	Adds a graphic you save in a CGM file to the worksheet when you specify a file with a CGM extension, and then specify the range in which you want the graphic to appear.

Menu Item	Description
Blank	Adds a blank graphic placeholder to the worksheet when you specify the range in which you want the graphic to appear.

Notes

1-2-3 sizes the graphic to fit in the specified range.

If you are designing a worksheet and know where you want to add a graphic but don't yet have the 1-2-3 graph or graphic metafile, use :Graph Add Blank to add a blank placeholder the size of the graphic you will eventually add. After you are ready to place the graphic, use :Graph Settings Graph to replace the blank placeholder with the graphic.

:Graph Compute

Purpose

Updates all graphics in the worksheet.

To update graphics

Select :Graph Compute.

Note

1-2-3 updates current and named 1-2-3 graphs and blank placeholders with every worksheet recalculation, unless you change the default with :Graph Settings Sync No.

:Graph Edit

Purpose

Places the graphic you added to the worksheet by using :Graph Add to the graphics editing window. You then can edit and enhance the graphic by using the :Graph Edit commands.

> **Reminders:** You must be in graphics display mode to use the :Graph Edit commands.
>
> You must select, or identify, objects and underlying graphics in the graphics editing window to edit, move, rearrange, or transform them with the :Graph Edit commands. Select objects with the :Graph Edit Select commands or the mouse.

To edit a graphic

1. Select :Graph Edit.

2. Select the graphic you want to edit by specifying a cell in the range that the graphic occupies or by pressing F3 (Name) and selecting the graphic from the list that appears.

3. Select one of the following options:

Menu Item	Description
Add	Adds objects, such as text, geometric shapes, and freehand drawings to a graphic.
Select	Selects an object, group of objects, or graphic to edit in the graphics editing window.

Menu Item	Description
Edit	Enables you to modify the appearance of objects you add to a graphic.
Color	Specifies colors for a graphic and objects you add to a graphic.
Transform	Changes orientation or size of a graphic and the objects you add to the graphic.
Rearrange	Copies, moves, deletes and restores, locks and unlocks, and determines the place-ment (front or back) of objects you add to a graphic.
View	Enlarges and reduces areas of the graphics editing window.
Options	In the graphics editing window, adds grid lines, changes the size of the cursor, or magnifies fonts.

Many of these commands require you to move a cursor that appears on-screen after issuing a command. Use the direction keys or the mouse to move the cursor.

Some commands require anchoring after mov-ing the cursor. Use the space bar or left mouse button to anchor the cursor. Press Enter or double-click the left mouse button to complete the operation.

Notes

You can move a graphic to the graphics editing window from READY mode by double-clicking a graphic with the left mouse button.

To add a cell's contents in a file to a graphic by using :Graph Edit Add Text, type \ (backslash), the cell's name or address, and press Enter. If you enter a multicell range name or address, Wysiwyg adds the contents of the first cell in the range.

You can position an object to add to a graphic by using x- and y-coordinates as anchor points. Rather than using the mouse or direction keys to move the cursor to a location, type x,y where x is an x-coordinate from 0 to 4095 and y is a y-coordinate from 0 to 4095.

To add a line of text or anchor the first point of a line, polygon, rectangle, ellipse, or freehand drawing, click the left mouse button or press the space bar. To complete a line, polygon, rectangle, ellipse, or freehand drawing, double-click the left mouse button or press Enter.

To leave the :Graph Edit menu, choose Quit. All changes made in the graphics editing window appear in the graph in the worksheet.

:Graph Goto

Purpose

Moves the cell pointer to a specific graphic in the worksheet.

To move the cell pointer to a graphic

1. Select :Graph Goto.

2. At the prompt, type the graphic's name, highlight the name of the graphic and press Enter, or type a cell address that lies in the range the graphic occupies and press Enter.

:Graph Move

Purpose

Moves a graphic to another range in the worksheet.

To move a graphic

1. Select :Graph Move.

2. To select the graphic you want to move, specify a cell in the range that the graphic occupies, or press F3 (Name) and select the graphic from the list that appears on-screen.

3. At the prompt, specify the first cell of the new range for the graphic and press Enter.

Notes

:Graph Move doesn't change the number of rows and columns in the range that the graphic occupies. If you move the graphic to a range that contains different row heights or column widths, however, 1-2-3 resizes the graphic to fit in the new range.

:Graph Move doesn't affect data that may lie beneath the graphic you move to another range.

:Graph Remove

Purpose

Deletes a graphic from the worksheet.

Reminder: :Graph Remove doesn't delete the actual named graph, graph file, graphic metafile, or current graph settings from memory or from disk and also doesn't affect data that may be beneath the graphic you delete from the worksheet.

To delete a graphic

1. Select :Graph Remove.

2. To select the graphic you want to remove, enter a cell address in the range that the graphic occupies, or press F3 (Name) and select the graphic from the list that 1-2-3 displays.

3. Press Enter.

Notes

To specify more than one graphic to remove, specify a range that contains more than one graphic.

If you use :Graph Remove to delete a graphic from the worksheet, you lose all enhancements made to the graphic with the :Graph Edit commands.

:Graph Settings

Purpose

Moves, resizes, and replaces graphics in the worksheet, turns on or off the display of graphics, makes graphics in the worksheet transparent or opaque, and updates 1-2-3 graphs in the worksheet when the data on which the graphs are based changes.

To specify graph settings

1. Select :Graph Settings.

2. Select one of the following options:

Menu Item	Description
Graph	Replaces a graphic in the worksheet with another graphic. After you specify the graphic you want to replace, select one of the following options:

Menu Item	Description
	Current replaces the specified graphic with the current graph.
	Named replaces the specified graphic with a named graph.
	PIC replaces the specified graphic with a 1-2-3 graph saved in a PIC file.
	Metafile replaces the specified graphic with a graphic saved in a CGM file.
	Blank replaces the specified graphic with a blank placeholder.
Range	Resizes the range a graphic occupies or moves a graphic in the worksheet to a specified range and, optionally, resizes the graphic.
Sync	Controls whether a graph is updated by default to reflect changes in the data on which the graph is based. Yes updates a named or current graph in the worksheet; No turns off the feature.
Display	Yes displays a selected graphic in the worksheet; No displays a selected graphic as shaded rectangles in the worksheet.

continues

Menu Item	Description
Opaque	Yes hides worksheet data underneath a selected graphic; No displays worksheet data underneath a selected graphic so that both the graphic and the data appear.

3. Select a graphic by specifying a cell in the range that the graphic occupies or by pressing F3 (Name) and selecting the graphic from the list that 1-2-3 displays.

   To specify more than one graphic, specify a range that contains more than one graphic.

4. To resize the graphic, use the mouse or direction keys to adjust the size of the range, and then press Enter.

Notes

If you use :Graph Edit Color Background to make the color of the range the graphic occupies transparent, 1-2-3 displays nothing in the worksheet when you select :Graph Settings Display No.

:Graph Settings Graph removes no enhancements you added with the :Graph Edit commands. To replace a graphic and the graph's enhancements, use :Graph Remove to remove the graphic and enhancements from the worksheet; then use :Graph Add to add a different graphic.

:Graph View

Purpose

Removes the worksheet from the screen temporarily and enables you to display on-screen a graphic that was saved in a PIC or CGM file.

To display a graphic

1. Select :Graph View.
2. Select one of the following options:

Menu Item	Description
PIC	Displays a list of 1-2-3 graphs that are saved in PIC format.
Metafile	Displays a list of graphics that are saved in CGM format.

3. Select the graphic you want to display and press Enter. You see a full-screen display of the graphic.
4. When you finish viewing the graphic, press any key to remove it and redisplay the worksheet.

:Graph Zoom

Purpose

Removes the worksheet from the screen temporarily and displays on-screen a specified graphic in the worksheet.

To zoom a worksheet graphic on-screen

1. Select :Graph Zoom.
2. To specify the graphic to display on-screen, specify a cell in the range the graphic occupies, or press F3 (Name) and select the graphic from the list 1-2-3 displays.
3. After you finish viewing the graphic, press any key to redisplay the worksheet.

:Named-Style

Purpose

Defines a named style or collection of Wysiwyg
formats taken from a single cell, and then applies
the named style to one or more ranges in the
current file.

Reminder: Each file can contain up to eight
named styles.

To define and apply a style

1. Select :Named-Style.
2. Select one of the following options:

Menu Item	Description
1 through 8	Formats one or more ranges with the named styles previously defined with :Named-Style Define.
Define	Creates a named style of the Wysiwyg formats in a specified cell to apply to other cells that require the same formats.

3. For :Named-Style 1 through :Named-Style 8,
   specify the cell or range to which you want to
   apply the selected style, and then press Enter.

   For :Named-Style Define, choose from 1
   through 8, highlight or type the cell to define,
   and then press Enter. Finally, type a description of up to 37 characters and press Enter.

Note

If you redefine a named style, 1-2-3 reformats all ranges formatted with the named style.

:Print Background

Purpose

Prints data from an encoded file while enabling you to continue to work in 1-2-3.

Reminder: After the file has printed, 1-2-3 deletes the encoded file.

You must load the BPRINT utility program before you can use /Print Background. For more information, refer to Que's *Using 1-2-3 Release 2.4,* Special Edition or the Lotus documentation.

To print in the background

1. Use :Print Range Set, define the range you want to print, and press Enter.
2. Select Background.
3. Type a name for the encoded file and press Enter. If the file already exists, select Cancel to return to 1-2-3 without creating the file, or select Replace to write over the existing file.

:Print Config

Purpose

Specifies the printer, printer interface, font cartridges, orientation, and paper-feed method.

To specify print configuration options

1. Select :Print Config.
2. Select one of the following options:

Menu Item	Description
Printer	Selects the printer on which to print a specified range.
Interface	Specifies the interface or port that connects the computer to the printer.
1st-Cart	Specifies a font cartridge or font card for the printer to use when you select a font-cartridge file or font-card file.
2nd-Cart	Specifies a second font cartridge or font card for the printer to use when you select a second font-cartridge file or font-card file.
Orientation	Determines whether Wysiwyg prints in Portrait mode or Landscape mode. (To use the Landscape option, landscape mode must be available on the printer.)
Bin	Specifies the paper-feed option for the printer. You can choose from the following options:
	Reset clears the current bin setting.
	Single-Sheet specifies the single-sheet feeder.

Menu Item	Description
	Manual specifies manual form-feed.
	Upper-Tray specifies the top paper tray.
	Lower-Tray specifies the bottom paper tray.

:Print File

Purpose

Prints a range to an encoded file. The file can include 1-2-3 data, graphics, and printer codes for all Wysiwyg options, such as fonts, colors, line spacing, and print compression. The printer codes Wysiwyg uses are specific to your current printer.

Reminder: You cannot read an encoded file back into 1-2-3.

To print a range to an encoded file

1. Select :Print Range Set, specify a print range, and then press Enter.
2. Select File.
3. Type a name for the encoded file and press Enter.
4. If you are updating an existing encoded file, select Cancel to return to READY mode without saving an encoded file.

   To overwrite the encoded file on disk with the current file, select Replace.

Note

Wysiwyg adds the extension ENC to encoded files unless you specify a different extension.

:Print Go

Purpose

Sends data to a printer.

To send data to a printer

1. Select :Print Range Set, specify a print range, and press Enter.

2. Verify that the printer is on-line and the paper is at the top of a page.

3. Select Go. The data prints.

:Print Info

Purpose

Removes or redisplays the Wysiwyg print settings sheet that overlays the worksheet when you select :Print.

To remove or display the Wysiwyg print settings sheet

Select :Print Info.

Note

You also can press F6 (Window) to remove or display the Wysiwyg print settings sheet when you are using the :Print menu.

:Print Layout

Purpose
Controls the page layout, or the overall positioning and appearance of the page.

> **Reminder:** 1-2-3 saves page layout settings for a worksheet file in the corresponding format file.

To set the page layout settings
1. Select :Print Layout.
2. Select one of the following options:

Menu Item	Description
Page-Size	Specifies the length and width of the page when you select from page sizes numbered 1 through 7. Custom enables you to enter a number for page length and a number for page width in inches (in) or millimeters (mm).
Margins	Sets Left, Right, Top, and Bottom margins when you enter a number followed by in (inches) or mm (millimeters) and press Enter.
Titles	Creates page headers and footers by using the Header and Footer commands and clears headers and footers with the Clear Header, Clear Footer, or Clear Both commands.

continues

Menu Item	Description
Borders	Top specifies one or more rows to print at the top of every page and above all print ranges. Left specifies one or more columns to print at the left of every page and print range. Clear Top, Clear Left, or Clear All clears the borders you set.
Compression	Compresses or expands a print range, so that more or less text fits on a page. You can choose from the following options:

None removes compression or expansion from a print range.

Manual compresses the print range when you type a number from 15 to 99 and press Enter; expands the print range when you type a number from 101 to 1000 and press Enter. The default setting for no compression is 100.

Automatic compresses a print range by default, up to a factor of seven, by fitting the range on one printed page when possible. |
| Default | Sets the default page layout setting. Update creates a new default page layout setting; Restore replaces a current page layout setting with the default page layout setting. |

Menu Item	Description
Library	Enables you to Retrieve, Save, or Erase page layout libraries on disk after you specify the name of the page layout library file.

3. If you select :Print Layout Page-Size Custom, enter numbers in inches by typing the number followed by in, and then press Enter. You can enter numbers in millimeters by typing the number followed by mm, and then press Enter.

   If you select :Print Layout Titles Header or :Print Layout Titles Footer, type the header or footer at the prompt and press Enter.

   If you select :Print Layout Borders Top, :Print Layout Borders Left, or :Print Layout Borders Clear, specify a range that includes the rows or columns you want to use as a border.

   If you select :Print Layout Library Save to update an existing layout library, select Cancel to return 1-2-3 to READY mode without saving the current layout library. Select Replace to overwrite the layout library on disk with the current layout library.

Notes

Type cm to denote a setting in centimeters; Wysiwyg converts the setting to millimeters automatically.

Don't include in the print range the rows and columns you specify as borders, or Wysiwyg prints these rows and columns twice.

Wysiwyg prints headers on the line below the top margin and footers on the line above the bottom margin. Wysiwyg always leaves two blank lines measured in the default font between printed data and the header or footer.

Wysiwyg uses four symbols to format headers and footers: # (pound sign) for page numbers, @ (at sign) for the current date, | (vertical bar) for alignment, and \ (backslash) to copy cell contents.

:Print Preview

Purpose
Removes the worksheet from the screen temporarily and displays the print range as Wysiwyg formats the range for printing, page by page.

To display the print range on-screen in the same way as on a printed page
1. Select :Print Preview.
2. Press any key (except Esc) to cycle through the pages. Press Esc to redisplay the worksheet.

:Print Range

Purpose
Specifies or cancels the print range. The print range is the data Wysiwyg prints when you select :Print Go, :Print File, or :Print Background.

To specify or cancel a print range
1. Select :Print Range.
2. Select Set to specify the print range. Select Clear to clear the settings for the current print range.

   If you select Set, specify the print range to set and press Enter.

Notes

If the print range includes a long label, include in the print range the cells that the long label overlaps and also the cell in which you entered the long label.

In graphics display mode, the boundaries of the print range appear as dashed lines along the edges of the print range. The dashed lines remain on-screen until you use :Print Range Clear to clear the print range.

:Print Settings

Purpose

Specifies which pages of a print range to print, the number of copies to print, whether to print the worksheet frame and grid lines, and whether to pause for manual paper feed. :Print Settings also controls page numbering and enables you to select the page number of the first page.

> Reminder: The Wysiwyg print settings are separate from the 1-2-3 print settings and, except for the Frame and Grid settings, affect only the current Wysiwyg session.

To specify print settings

1. Select :Print Settings.
2. Select one of the following options:

Menu Item	Description
Begin	Specifies the page number at which printing begins.
End	Specifies the last page to print.

continues

Menu Item	Description
Start-Number	Specifies the page number of the first page in the print range.
Copies	Specifies the number of copies to print.
Wait	Specifies if printing pauses after each page. If you select No, printing doesn't pause after each page. If you select Yes, printing pauses after each page.
Grid	Specifies if the worksheet grid lines print with the print range. If you select No, the worksheet grid lines don't print. If you select Yes, the worksheet grid lines print.
Frame	Specifies if the worksheet frame prints with the print range. If you select No, the worksheet frame doesn't print. If you select Yes, the worksheet frame prints.
Reset	Returns the Wysiwyg print settings to the defaults.

If you select Begin, End, Start-Number, or Copies, type the appropriate page number, or number of copies to print, and press Enter.

If you select Wait Yes, Wysiwyg prompts you to insert the next sheet of paper after each page is printed. Insert the next sheet of paper and press any key to resume printing, or press Esc to cancel.

Notes

The beginning and ending page numbers depend on the page numbering you specify with :Print Settings Start-Number.

Wysiwyg prints the standard 1-2-3 worksheet frame regardless of how you set up the worksheet frame, using :Display Options Frame.

:Quit

Purpose

Returns 1-2-3 to READY mode from Wysiwyg mode.

To return to READY mode

Select :Quit.

Note

To exit 1-2-3, select /Quit.

:Special Copy

Purpose

Copies all Wysiwyg formats in one range to another range.

Reminder: :Special Copy doesn't copy data, graphics in the worksheet, or 1-2-3 formats you set with the /Range Format or /Worksheet Global Format commands.

To copy Wysiwyg formats

1. Select :Special Copy.

2. Specify the range from which you want to copy formats and press Enter.

3. Specify the range to which you want to copy formats and press Enter.

:Special Export

Purpose

Creates a file with the font set, formats, named styles, and graphics in a Wysiwyg format file (FMT extension) or Allways format file (ALL extension).

To export to a Wysiwyg format file

1. Select :Special Export.

2. Specify the format file to which you want to export and press Enter.

3. If you are updating an existing format file, select Cancel to return 1-2-3 to READY mode without exporting the current format file. Select Replace to write over the format file on disk with a copy of the current format file.

Notes

1-2-3 exports to a Wysiwyg format file (FMT) automatically unless you enter a different extension. To export to an Allways format file, enter the extension ALL.

If the file from which you export contains current or named graphs, 1-2-3 exports only their positions in the worksheet and enhancements made with the :Graph Edit commands, not the graphs.

Many Wysiwyg features are unavailable in Allways and are therefore lost when saved in an Allways format file (ALL).

:Special Import

Purpose

Applies the formats, named styles, font set, and graphics from a Wysiwyg format file (FMT) or Allways format file (ALL) on disk to the current file.

Reminder: 1-2-3 imports from a Wysiwyg format file (FMT) automatically unless you enter a different extension. To import from an Allways format file, enter the extension ALL.

To import from a Wysiwyg format file

1. Select :Special Import.

2. Select one of the following options:

Menu Item	Description
All	Replaces all formats, named styles, and graphics in the current file with the formats, named styles, and graphics from a format file on disk.
Named-Styles	Replaces the named styles in the current file with the named styles from a Wysiwyg or Allways format file on disk.
Fonts	Replaces the font set in the current file with the font set from a format file on disk.

continues

Menu Item	Description
Graphs	Copies graphics, including their positions in the worksheet and all enhancements you add with the :Graph Edit commands, from a format file on disk to the current file.

3. Specify a format file from which to import and press Enter.

Notes

:Special Import Graphs doesn't delete any graphic you have already added to the current file with :Graph Add.

If you import current or named graphs, 1-2-3 imports only the positions in the worksheet and enhancements you made with the :Graph Edit commands, not the graphs.

:Special Move

Purpose

Transfers the format of one range to another range and causes the cells that originally contained the formats to revert to the default formats. This command doesn't move data, graphics, or 1-2-3 formats set with the /Range Format or /Worksheet Global Format commands.

To move a range format

1. Select :Special Move.
2. Specify the range from which you want to move formats and press Enter.
3. Specify the range to which you want to move formats and press Enter.

Note

The formats of the range from which you moved return to the defaults.

:Text Align

Purpose

Changes the alignment of labels within a text range by changing their label prefixes.

To change the alignment of labels

1. Select :Text Align.
2. Select one of the following:

Menu Item	Description
Left	Aligns labels with the left edge of the text range.
Right	Aligns labels with the right edge of the text range.
Center	Centers labels in the text range.
Even	Aligns labels with both the left and right edges of the text range.

3. Specify the range within which you want to align labels and press Enter.

:Text Clear

Purpose

Clears the settings for a text range, but doesn't erase the data or alignment contained in the range or change any formatting performed on the data with the :Text Reformat or :Text Edit commands.

To clear the settings for a text range

1. Select :Text Clear.

2. Specify the text range whose settings you want to clear and press Enter.

Note

After you use :Text Clear, the formatting description {Text} no longer appears in the control panel when the cell pointer is in the original text range.

:Text Edit

Purpose

Enables you to enter and edit labels in a text range directly in the worksheet.

To enter and edit labels in a specified range

1. Select :Text Edit.

2. Specify the range in which you want to edit text and press Enter.

   Wysiwyg goes into TEXT mode and you can type data in the range. When you reach the end of a line, the cursor jumps to the next line.

3. When you finish typing or editing, press Esc to return 1-2-3 to READY mode.

Notes

When you issue the :Text Edit command, a cursor appears at the first character in the range and the mode indicator changes to TEXT.

:Text Edit permits you to enter text only in the range you specify but doesn't place text in rows not included in the specified range.

You can press F3 when using :Text Edit to display a menu of formatting options that you can apply to text you enter or edit.

On-screen graphics are displayed as shaded rectangles while in TEXT mode.

:Text Reformat

Purpose

Rearranges (justifies) a column of labels so that the labels fit within a text range.

Reminders: To use :Text Reformat, you must turn off global protection for the worksheet.

Using :Text Reformat on cells whose contents are used in formulas might change or invalidate the results of the formulas.

To justify a column of labels

1. Move the cell pointer to the first cell in the column of labels you want to rearrange.

2. Select :Text Reformat.

3. Specify the text range in which you want to rearrange labels and press Enter.

Notes

:Text Reformat affects labels only in the first column of a text range.

When Wysiwyg rearranges the text, all labels within the range are aligned, depending on the prefix of the first label.

:Text Set

Purpose

Specifies a text range so that you can use the :Text commands with labels in the range.

To specify a text range

1. Select :Text Set.

2. Specify the range you want to make a text range and press Enter.

Note

After you use :Text Set, the formatting description {Text} appears in the control panel when the cell pointer is in the text range.

:Worksheet Column

Purpose

Sets the width of one or more columns and resets columns to the 1-2-3 global column width.

Reminder: The column widths you specify remain in effect even after you remove Wysiwyg from memory.

To set the width of one or more columns

1. Select :Worksheet Column.

2. Select Set-Width to set the column width for one or more columns. Select Reset-Width to reset one or more columns to the global column width.

3. Depending on your choice in step 2, take one of the following actions:

    If you select Set-Width, specify the range of columns whose widths you want to set. Specify the new width by typing a number from 1 to 240 and pressing Enter, or by pressing ← or →, and then pressing Enter.

    If you select Reset-Width, specify the range of columns whose widths you want to reset to the global column width, and then press Enter.

Notes

When the screen is split into two horizontal or vertical windows, the :Worksheet Column commands affect only the window in which the cell pointer is located. When you clear the windows, 1-2-3 uses the top or left column settings of the window.

If you set the display of a worksheet frame by using :Display Options Frame [Enhanced, Relief], you can use the mouse to set the width of a column when 1-2-3 is in READY mode. You also can use the mouse to hide or redisplay a column when 1-2-3 is in READY mode or if Frame is set to 1-2-3. You can set the width of a column that has the cell pointer.

:Worksheet Page

Purpose

Inserts or removes horizontal or vertical page breaks that tell 1-2-3 to begin a new page when printing with the Wysiwyg :Print commands.

To insert or remove page breaks

1. Position the cell pointer in the leftmost column or top row on which you want to begin a new page.
2. Select :Worksheet Page.
3. Select one of the following options:

Menu Item	Description
Row	Inserts a horizontal page break.
Column	Inserts a vertical page break.
Delete	Removes page breaks—vertical, horizontal, or both—from the current column, row, or both.

Notes

1-2-3 inserts a dashed line along the left of the column for a vertical page break or along the top of the row for a horizontal page break. When you print data, 1-2-3 begins a new page at the row or column you specify.

To hide the dashed lines that symbolize page breaks on-screen, use :Display Options Page-Breaks No.

:Worksheet Row

Purpose

Sets the height of one or more rows. You can specify a height in points, or make 1-2-3 set row heights automatically to accommodate the largest font in a row.

To specify row height

1. Select :Worksheet Row.

2. Select Set-Height to set the row height for one or more rows. Select Auto to set the height of one or more rows automatically based on the size of the largest font in each row.

3. Depending on your choice in step 2, take one of the following actions:

   If you select Set-Height, specify the range of rows whose heights you want to set. You then can specify the row height by typing a number from 1 to 255 and pressing Enter, or by pressing ↑ and ↓, and then pressing Enter.

   If you select Auto, specify the range of rows whose heights you want 1-2-3 to set, based on the font, and then press Enter.

Note

If you use :Display Options Frame [1-2-3 Enhanced, Relief] to set the display of the worksheet frame,

you can use the mouse to set the height of a row
when 1-2-3 is in READY mode. You also can use the
mouse to hide or redisplay a row when in READY
mode.

1-2-3 RELEASE 2.4 ADD-INS

The 1-2-3 Release 2.4 add-ins—Auditor, Backsolver,
Macro Library Manager, SmartIcons, Tutor, Viewer,
and Wysiwyg—are attached to 1-2-3 with the /Add-In
command.

Note

By default, Wysiwyg and SmartIcons add-ins are
automatically attached when you start 1-2-3 Release
2.4. In Release 2.3 you must attach the Wysiwyg
add-in (the SmartIcons add-in is unavailable in
Release 2.3).

To select and attach an add-in

1. Select /Add-In Attach.

   A list of add-ins appears.

2. Highlight the desired add-in and press Enter.

3. If you don't want to assign a function key to
   the add-in, select No-Key.

4. To assign a function key to the add-in, select
   7, 8, 9, or 10.

   The preceding numbers correspond to function keys Alt-F7, Alt-F8, Alt-F9, and Alt-F10.

5. To return to the 1-2-3 worksheet, select Quit.

Note

You can use the /Worksheet Global Default Other
Add-In Set command to load an add-in automatically
each time you start 1-2-3.

The Auditor Add-In

Purpose

Helps analyze worksheets to ensure accuracy. Shows how formula and data cells relate, order of recalculation, and circular references.

Reminder: Before you can use the Auditor commands, you must attach and then invoke the Auditor add-in by pressing the assigned function key.

To use Auditor

The following options are available when you invoke Auditor add-in:

Menu Item	Description
Circs	Locates and identifies circular references
Dependents	Identifies all cells that depend on the value of a specified cell
Formulas	Identifies all formulas in the audit range
Options	Enables you to specify the following Auditor settings:
	Highlight highlights all matching cells
	List generates a list (in the specified worksheet range) of matching cells
	Trace moves the cell pointer to matching cells
	Audit-Range specifies the area you want to audit. The default range is the entire worksheet

Menu Item	Description
	Reset Highlight removes highlights previously added by Auditor
	Reset Options returns all options to default settings
Precedents	Identifies cells on which a specified cell depends
Recalc-List	Identifies the order in which formulas are recalculated

The Backsolver Add-In

Purpose

Changes the value of one or more variables to produce a desired end result.

Reminder: Before you can use the Backsolver commands, you must attach the Backsolver add-in, and then invoke it by pressing the assigned function key.

To use the Backsolver

The following options are available when you attach and invoke Backsolver:

Menu Item	Description
Adjustable	Specifies the value you want to change
Formula-Cell	Specifies the formula that should equal a specified value

continues

Menu Item	Description
Solve	Solves the specified problem
Value	Specifies value the formula should equal

The Macro Library Manager Add-In

Purpose

Enables you to use macros in any worksheet without storing them in each file. Because the macros are in memory but not in the worksheet, you don't need to worry about accidentally deleting the macros when you delete rows or columns in the worksheet.

Reminder: Before you can use the Macro Library Manager commands, you must attach and then invoke the Macro Library Manager add-in by pressing the assigned function key.

To use the Macro Library Manager

The following options are available when you attach and invoke the Macro Library Manager Add-in:

Menu Item	Description
Edit	Copies a macro library from memory to the worksheet
Load	Makes the macros in a library accessible in any worksheet
Name-List	Lists the range names stored in a macro library in memory

Menu Item	Description
Remove	Erases a macro library from memory (but not from disk)
Save	Moves the macros in the worksheet into a macro library file and into memory.

The Viewer Add-In

Purpose

Enables you to examine files before retrieving or opening them. Greatly simplifies the creation of file-linking formulas.

Reminder: Before you can use the Viewer commands, you must attach and then invoke the Viewer add-in by pressing the assigned function key.

To use the Viewer

The following options are available when you attach and invoke the Viewer add-in:

Browse	Enables you to view the contents of text files.
Link	Displays worksheet files, creates formulas in the current worksheet that link the current worksheet to the displayed file
Retrieve	Displays and retrieves a worksheet file (replacing the current file)

1-2-3 @FUNCTIONS

This section provides all 1-2-3 @functions in alphabetical order. For an in-depth discussion of 1-2-3 @functions, see Que's *Using 1-2-3 Release 2.4*, Special Edition.

@@(*cell_reference*)

@?

@ABS(*number*)

@ACOS(*x*)

@ASIN(*x*)

@ATAN(*x*)

@ATAN2(*x,y*)

@AVG(*list*)

@CELL(*attribute,range*)

@CELLPOINTER(*attribute*)

@CHAR(*number*)

@CHOOSE(*offset,list*)

@CLEAN(*string*)

@CODE(*string*)

@COLS(*range*)

@COS(*x*)

@COUNT(*list*)

@CTERM(*interest,future_value,present_value*)

@DATE(*year,month,day*)

@DATEVALUE(*date_string*)

@DAVG(*input_range,offset,criteria_range*)

@DAY(*date*)

@DCOUNT(*input_range,offset,criteria_range*)

@DDB(*cost,salvage,life,period*)

@DMAX(*input_range,offset,criteria_range*)

@DMIN(*input_range,offset,criteria_range*)

@DSTD(*input_range,offset,criteria_range*)

@DSUM(*input_range,offset,criteria_range*)

@DVAR(*input_range,offset,criteria_range*)

@ERR

@EXACT(*string1,string2*)

@EXP(*number*)

@FALSE

@FIND(*search_string,string,start_number*)

@FV(*payment,interest,term*)

@HLOOKUP(*key,range,row_offset*)

@HOUR(*time*)

@IF(*test,true,false*)

@INDEX(*range,column,row*)

@INT(*number*)

@IRR(*guess,cashflows*)

@ISAAF(*name*)

@ISAPP(*name*)

@ISERR(*x*)

@ISNA(*x*)

@ISNUMBER(*x*)

@ISSTRING(*x*)

@LEFT(*string,number*)

@LENGTH(*string*)

@LN(*number*)

@LOG(*number*)

@LOWER(*string*)

@MAX(*list*)

@MID(*string,start_number,number*)

@MIN(*list*)

@MINUTE(*time*)

@MOD(*number,divisor*)

@MONTH(*date*)

@N(*range*)

@NA

@NOW

continues

@NPV(*interest,cashflows*)

@PI

@PMT(*principal,interest,term*)

@PROPER(*string*)

@PV(*payment,interest,term*)

@RAND

@RATE(*future_value,present_value,term*)

@REPEAT(*string,number*)

@REPLACE(*original_string,start_number,
    length,replacement_string*)

@RIGHT(*string,number*)

@ROUND(*number,precision*)

@ROWS(*range*)

@S(*range*)

@SECOND(*time*)

@SIN(*x*)

@SLN(*cost,salvage,life*)

@SQRT(*number*)

@STD(*list*)

@STRING(*number,decimal_places*)

@SUM(*list*)

@SYD(*cost,salvage,life,period*)

@TAN(*x*)

@TERM(*payment,interest,future_value*)

@TIME(*hour,minute,second*)

@TIMEVALUE(*time_string*)

@TODAY

@TRIM(*string*)

@TRUE

@UPPER(*string*)

@VALUE(*string*)

@VAR(*list*)

@VLOOKUP(*key,range,column_offset*)

@YEAR(*date*)

MACRO KEY NAMES

Macro key names automate single- or multiple-key activities (such as Home, End, or Shift-Tab) within macros. Using {HOME} in a macro, for example, moves the cell pointer to the upper left corner of the worksheet. Use the following macro key names to perform the indicated key presses. Optional arguments are enclosed within square brackets.

Macro Key Name	Keyboard Name
~	Enter
{~}	Enters ~ (tilde)
{{}	Enters { (open brace)
{}}	Enters } (close brace)
{ABS [number]}	F4 (Abs)
{APP1}	Alt-F7 (App1)
{APP2}	Alt-F8 (App2)
{APP3}	Alt-F9 (App3)
{APP4}	Alt-F10 (App4)
{BS[number]}	Backspace
{BIGLEFT [number]}	Shift-Tab or Ctrl ←
{BIGRIGHT [number]}	Tab or Ctrl →
{CALC [number]}	F9 (Calc)
{DELETE [number]} or {DEL [number]}	Del
{DOWN [number]} or {D [number]}	↓
{EDIT}	F2 (Edit)
{END}	End

continues

Macro Key Name	Keyboard Name
{ESCAPE [*number*]} or {ESC [*number*]}	Esc
{GOTO}	F5 (GoTo)
{GRAPH}	F10 (Graph)
{HELP}	F1 (Help)
{HOME}	Home
{INSERT} or {INS}	Ins
{LEFT [*number*]} or {L [*number*]}	←
{MENU}	/ (slash) or < (less than)
{NAME [*number*]}	F3 (Name)
{PGDN [*number*]}	PgDn
{PGUP [*number*]}	PgUp
{QUERY}	F7 (Query)
{RIGHT [*number*]} or {R [*number*]}	→
{TABLE}	F8 (Table)
{UP [*number*]} or {U [*number*]}	↑
{WINDOW}	F6 (Window)

ADVANCED MACRO COMMANDS

This section provides all 1-2-3 advanced macro commands in alphabetical order. Optional arguments are enclosed in square brackets. For a discussion of 1-2-3 advanced macro commands, see Que's *Using 1-2-3 Release 2.4*, Special Edition.

{?}

{APPENDBELOW *destination,source*}

{APPENDRIGHT *destination,source*}

{BEEP [*tone_number*]}

{BLANK *location*}

{BORDERSOFF}

{BORDERSON}

{BRANCH *location*}

{BREAK}

{BREAKOFF}

{BREAKON}

{CLOSE}

{CONTENTS *destination,source,*[*width*]*,*[*format*]}

{DEFINE *loc1*[*:type1*]*,...,locN*[*:typeN*]}

{DISPATCH *location*}

{FILESIZE *location*}

{FOR *counter,start,stop,step,subroutine*}

{FORBREAK}

{FORM *input,*[*call_table*]*,*
    [*include_keys*]*,*[*exclude_keys*]}

{FORMBREAK}

{FRAMEOFF}

{FRAMEON}

{GET *location*}
{GETLABEL *prompt,location*}
{GETNUMBER *prompt,location*}
{GETPOS *location*}
{GRAPHOFF}
{GRAPHON [*named_graph*],[nodisplay]}
{IF *condition*}
{INDICATE [*string*]}
{LET *location,expression*}
{LOOK *location*}
{MENUBRANCH *location*}
{MENUCALL *location*}
{ONERROR *branch,*[*message*]}
{OPEN *filename,access_mode*}
{PANELOFF [clear]}
{PANELON}
{PUT *range,col,row,value*}
{QUIT}
{READ *bytecount,location*}
{READLN *location*}
{RECALC *location,*[*condition*],[*iterations*]}
{RECALCCOL *location,*[*condition*],[*iterations*]}
{RESTART}
{RETURN}
{SETPOS *file_position*}
{*subroutine* [*arg1*],[*arg2*],...,[*argN*]}
{SYSTEM *command*}
{WAIT *argument*}
{WINDOWSOFF}
{WINDOWSON}
{WRITE *string*}
{WRITELN *string*}

INDEX

X-Y-Z